the transit of saturn

by marc robertson

ISBN Number 0-86690-149-3

Published By

AMERICAN FEDERATION OF ASTROLOGERS, INC.

Movements of bodies in the sky around us can
be considered to be the communication of the WHOLE
(the psychological solar system) with its PARTS (us).
There is little to fear from them but the ridiculous super-
stitions built around them.

Every sign of the Zodiac is operating somewhere in every person.
Each sign represents an attitude to, and a need from, life.
Saturn's transit through the signs shows how the individual
defines, curbs and makes realistic his needs and attitudes.
INTERPRETATION of Saturn in the Signs, Pages 11-14.

Individual potential and its lifelong development for effective
operation in society, is determined by birth TIME, not
birth date. The Axis of the birth chart, dividing it into
four quadrants, determines the rhythm of
individual potential development in each person.

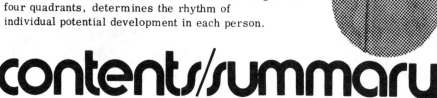

contents/summary

The movement of Saturn through the quadrants, and subsidiary
houses, of the birth chart coincides with major ups and downs
in the individual's life record. It structures the realities
he must face in social terms. INTERPRETATION of Saturn
moving through the quadrants of the birth chart and through the
houses making up each quadrant. Pages 24-34.

Saturn's transit over a birth planet does not conclude with its
passage through the sign in which the planet is located. The
conjunction is merely the BEGINNING of a 30-year period
of personality development. It is also the beginning of a shaping of activities represented by the house that the transited
planet rules in the birth chart.

The critical stages of adult life coincide with
Saturn's movement in relation to its own birth position.
Everyone faces them at approximately the same ages.
The dynamic and challenging ages follow the phases and aspects
of this 30-year cycle. Because of that, we can see that
certain ages are critical in all adult lives as well as in childhood. INTERPRETATION OF CRITICAL AGES, Pages 43-53.

Realistic living out of an individual's conscious inner
goals in life is determined by the placement of the Sun, at birth,
in relation to Saturn, at birth. Major goals are re-oriented
and made real or defeated with Saturn's transit of the birth Sun.
The ages at which this operates are not the same in every life.
INTERPRETATION of Saturn-Sun cycle. Pages 54-56.

Every planet in the birth chart represents some
function of the personality. Saturn's transit of each represents
a shaping, in realistic terms, of each part of the personality.
INTERPRETATIONS of Saturn transiting birth planets. Pages
59-72.

'you probably thought.

when you were 21 years old, that you had passed through life's major crises and were ready to move out into the adult world with a major plan and a central goal. What a depressing surprise, then, to discover around the age of 28, that everything formerly planned and secure, was suddenly tumbling around your head; that you had developed a pressing, pushing inner urge to become "somebody else."

what you'll find inside

Society doesn't prepare its children for the fact that real adulthood comes between 28 and 30--comes with a seething inner crisis that causes careers to crumble, marriages to fail and individuals to face the most serious "identity crisis" of their early years.

Much less does society prepare us for the further, yet even more vital fact, that at the age of 35 an individual is operating at the prime of his individual potential and is setting forth on creative directi ns that will build him success or failure around age 42--when another severe identity crisis will arrive; an identity crisis that is, for most people, unplanned and unexpected.

But all these things happen--on a relentless schedule that moves, step by step, from climax to resolution. . . or defeat.

Society has plotted, in complex detail, the growth of an individual from childhood to voting age. But it has done little, if anything, about plotting the predictable, and age-oriented, crises and growth steps of adulthood through maturity. Yet those crises are there and they ARE predictable. They move in a choreography that follows the cyclic motion of the outer planets in our Solar System. The much-battered, superstition-haunted, citadel of astrology has known these cycles for hundreds of years. Its practitioners, caught up in their own specialized and self-isolating language, have never made much sense of these cycles to the modern, psychology-oriented mind. But now, even people who may know nothing about the language of astrology are beginning to plot out, and write about, these cycles. The February 18, 1974 issue of New York Magazine carried a lead article on the subject by a writer who plans a book on it. Her discoveries agree substantially with what you will find in this astrology-oriented text on the Saturn transits.

It's unfortunate astrology has isolated itself from the majority of people, but even they are beginning to recognize what it often holds hidden within its own specialized language: that life is cyclic and the phases, if not the specific contents, of its cycle can be known in advance. If you know nothing about the astrological language, you can turn immediately to pages 44 through 49, read the underlined passages and probably find some highly recognizable experiences.

about the text:

The original editions of this book were put out hurriedly
in response to the sudden demands that were placed for it.
Because of that, there were many flaws in the original editions.
This current revision is an attempt to remedy some of them,
but it will probably take until a third edition to remedy them completely.

You probably should take note of some of those flaws, because a
number of them remain in the current edition which is partially
set from the original impressions.

Throughout the text, with the exception of the edited parts of this
one, there is a consistent mis-spelling of the words, "transiting"
and "transited." Both words should contain a single "t" before the
suffix, but instead they contain a double "t." For those who wonder,
the double "t" is, indeed, a mis-spelling, but perhaps an explainable
one since it is almost exclusively astrologers, and some others
concerned with phenomena in the sky, who ever use the word as a
verb form in the language. For that reason, one can refer to dozens
of dictionaries and not find a listing of the word as a verb form used
in the manner as astrologers use it.

There is another interesting idiosyncracy of astrology that the
author also tried to stamp out in his usage of the language. It
is almost exclusively astrologers who refer to an individual as a
"native." Most modern individuals would probably blanch at reference
to themselves in that word-form and ask, "Native of what?"
It is a good question because employment of the word native in
describing an individual is a rather archaic term, made popular
by astrological texts of virtually Medieval origin. The author
has attempted to abandon the term and substitute the word
"individual" or "person" for it. One may think he has his own
special idiosyncracy, however, when he finds that the author has
continually used the word "natal" throughout the text.
If one consults a dictionary, he will discover why. One of the
basic meanings of "natal" is: "of or pertaining to the time or place
of one's birth."

The word "native," however, has many meanings, one of which is,
"an original inhabitant of a place." And this is probably what most
people think of when the word comes to mind. Native refers mainly to
"place" of birth and not "time" of birth. Modern astrology is based
on the idea that time of birth is probably the most significant factor in
the main differences between people--a greater factor than place of
birth. Therefrom, if it interests you, are the reasons for some of
the language usages in this book. The rest is simple poor English.

In attempting to make astrology comprehensible to modern individuals who grow up in a world of letters and numbers, rather
than heiroglyphic symbols, the author has also rendered the standard
astrological pictorial symbols into numbers and letters, in many
works and tools. Because these works and tools are becoming
widely distributed, the number and letter symbols for planets,
signs and aspects have been incorporated into the margin
descriptions in this book. The cycle aspect numbers are described
on the inside back cover; the planetary letter symbols are used
next to the heiroglyphs and the sign letter symbols are used next
to the sign glyphs.

Transits are the movements of the planets in the sky outside yourself AFTER your birth. They show how you can relate yourself to the cycles and energies that are moving men in general at all times. These "transiting" planets simply represent centers of energy, in the Solar System, saying "this is the most appropriate thing to be doing now with THIS human substance." The "thing to be doing now" is the activity represented by the transiting planet. "This human substance" is what is present in anyone, represented by the SIGN of the Zodiac through which the planet is traveling. Depending upon the time of day one was born, he will be using "this human substance" (or sign) in a particular field of activities in his life (in one of the houses of his birth chart).

The planets, in the sky, represent appropriate activity now for everyone. They show where, in human nature, their kind of activity is appropriate by their sign location as they move through that sky. But that does not say how the individual (you, or anyone, because of the unique individuality shown in the properly calculated birth chart) will make specific use of the activity in his life. That will depend upon his total individual makeup and what it equipped him to do at birth (because of the total individuality represented in his birth chart calculated to day, time and place of birth).

For instance, as this is being written, the planet Saturn is moving (or transiting) in the sector of the sky astrology calls Gemini. This means that the human substance that gives one the ability to "extend yourself vividly into your surroundings to make connections upon which personal foundations can be built" (a universal, rather than specific, meaning of the sign Gemini) is being urged to "define itself, take form in reality and become more profound if possible" (a universal, rather than specific, meaning of the kind of activity represented by the energy-center, Saturn, as it moves through the sky).

But HOW will one make use of it INDIVIDUALLY? We will have to look at his birth makeup (written in astrological shorthand in his birth chart) and find WHERE he NATURALLY uses the ability to "extend yourself vividly into your surroundings in order to make the connections on which personal foundations can be built," and see what he has done with it and what that means to him in his own terms. This we will discover in the field of activity (the birth chart house) in which that substance (that sign Gemini) is present at birth for activation.

If there are any centers of energy (birth planets) located in that substance Gemini, they will also be compelled to "define" themselves (or feel the effect of the Saturn transit). If there are such energy-centers to be activated, they will be activated in the operation of this field (this birth chart house that is being transited). But other activities will feel the influence of what is being done here, as well. There will be a subsequent effect of the current transit in the house or houses that bear the sign or signs ruled by the planet that Saturn is transiting. What one does with the energy offered by Saturn, here where it is transiting by house, will later have a strong effect upon the house of the birth chart bearing the sign Capricorn (the sign transiting Saturn rules), too. The movements of the energy-center Saturn through the sky will ALWAYS have some kind of effect upon that field of activities in one's life which bears the sign Capricorn. This latter proposition, by the way, is true of any transiting planet. While it affects directly the planet in the birth chart (which rules a sign on some house of the chart), it also affects the house in the chart on whose cusp we find the sign that this transiting planet rules.

In order to see how one can best make use of the energy that is being thrown into his life by a transit, we have to see how he was structured to handle such energy at birth. In other words, we have to see how that planet (the one of the same name as the one we are considering by transit) was structured into his makeup at birth. We have to see where it was meant to be used in activities (where it is by house placement), where it was placed to contribute to overall growth (where it is located by quadrant of the chart) and how it was made to dispose of its kind of energy in his life (where it is located by phase and aspect in relation to all the other planets in the birth chart).

In the case of Saturn, we have to see how birth Saturn was placed in relation to the house structure of the birth chart and all the other planets located in that house structure, in order to see the individual's essential "defining power" (for that is what Saturn's placement at birth basically gives an individual--despite the common astrological description of its unfortunate tendency to "limit, restrict and frustrate." That description is somewhat idiotic. The "limitation, restriction and frustration" come only from the individual's inability to understand that he must "define" himself as an individual).

what a transit is

The foregoing is not necessary to get a grasp of the most striking things that occur to individuals during Saturn's transits, but it is necessary if one is going to see how the occurrences relate to the individual's complete life makeup. Most people will never understand their complete makeup, anyway, so the striking things are what tend to stand out in their lives. And those striking things coincide with Saturn's transit of the quadrant, house, sign and planets of the birth chart.

If we consider the moving planets in the sky as representing the wholeness of the Solar System telling each substance of Man (each sign of the Zodiac) that there is now appropriate this kind of activity (the action the moving planet calls for) in this particular substance (the sign in which the planet is moving), we will begin to see that the transits are not the fearsome things old astrological textbooks have made of them. Instead, they are simply messages from the outside, from the greater wholeness surrounding us all, saying to us, "it would be well for you to know that the totality is proceeding upon this basis at this time and if you will consider your own makeup, you can see how you, specifically, can contribute to the total movement." In other words, the wholeness of the system is providing energy for THIS activity now, in this particular substance in any man (this sign) WHEREVER it lies in each individual's own total makeup (where it lies within the whole birth chart, or which house and which planet, if any, in the individual birth chart bear that sign substance).

Since the transits show how the whole is operating now, and disposing the substance in all men to be affected by the energy of the transiting planet now, it is valuable for an individual to know WHEN, and WHERE, in his makeup, the substances (the signs) will be activated at any time. That is the major value of the astrological transits, for they won't tell an individual what to do specifically.

One can move WITH the activation of that substance or AGAINST it. He may be so constructed, at birth, that either would be natural. But what DOES happen coincident with the transit will be his own choice. Yet he will not be unaffected, because it is a thing that is happening in the substance (the sign) in everyone at the same time and that substance lies SOMEWHERE in the makeup of each individual (the difference, for everyone, is HOW it is structured into the many departments of the individual birth chart). It is being activated whether men like it or not. Their choice is what they will do about that.

What astrology can do for anyone is show him where in his makeup this substance lies, when activation will occur (when the transit will be effective), and how it tends to affect individuals (what the transit generally precipitates in individuals).

From an "ephemeris" (a table of the planets' daily movements in the sky, past and future, for any year or number of years), we can discover the when. From an individual's own birth chart we can discover the where (the field of activities in which it will occur for him). Considering the nature of the moving planet, and what it represents basically as an activator of any substance, or sign, we can determine how anyone will be affected--though the SPECIFIC "how" still lies in the total ramifications of his basic potential (how HE was constructed, at birth, to use the kind of energy represented by the planet we are considering in transit) and what he has done, so far, with that potential.

If we decide what each planet means when it is moving in a particular area of the sky and calling for activity in the corresponding substance of the individual, we will find that Saturn is saying, essentially, DEFINE YOURSELF HERE. Jupiter is saying EXPAND YOURSELF HERE. Mars is saying DESIRE OR INITIATE ACTIVITY HERE. We will find that the outer, slower-moving planets are saying, over longer periods of time, TRANSFORM YOURSELF (Uranus calls for this in some part of every birth makeup for about seven years of time); MAKE CONTACT WITH A GREATER WORLD OF PERCEPTION (Neptune calls for this in some department of life for about 13 years); and, INITIATE YOURSELF INTO A GREATER LIFE ROLE--THROUGH A REBIRTH OF CONSCIOUSNESS (Pluto virtually demands this, in unconscious, compulsive ways, for a 13-to-30-year period, in some department of the individual life). The Pluto transit period is variable in years because it moves through some signs of the Zodiac rapidly and through others very slowly.

Not only are these planets activating signs of the Zodiac (or substances of Man AND individuals) and corresponding houses in the birth chart (or fields of individual life activity); they are also activating "quadrants" of the birth chart and calling for long phases of the development of growth in personal functioning.

These quadrants of the individual birth chart are functional in a life because of the birth time of an individual. They were structured by it. When we look at

the birth chart, we see it divided into 12 minor sections and 4 major sections. Each major quadrant contains 3 minor divisions, or three of the twelve "houses," as they are called traditionally. These quadrants are formed by the axis of the horizon (Ascendant to Descendant) and meridian (M.C. to I.C. or 10th house to 4th house cusps).

These quadrants represent, as moving astrological factors activate them, the ability to GROW IN ESSENTIAL BEING, or, as it is sometimes described, a withdrawal from outer activity to grow inside oneself (when planets move in quadrant One, running counterclockwise from Ascendant to 4th house cusp).

the ability to GROW IN CAPACITY, often described as emergence from withdrawal and growth inside to self-expression and new experience (when planets move in quadrant Two, running counterclockwise from the 4th house cusp to the 7th);

the ability to GROW IN FUNCTIONING, move out into activity and the opportunity that lies in it (when planets move into quadrant Three, running counterclockwise from the 7th house cusp to the M. C. or 10th house cusp).

the ability to GROW IN INFLUENCE, or consolidate activity and get results from the opportunity that the previous quadrant transit provided (when planets move into quadrant Four, running counterclockwise from the M. C. or 10th house cusp to the Ascendant).

All the planets are moving SOMEWHERE in the sky (and calling forth appropriate activity in the corresponding sky in you) at all times.

In order to see, therefore, what the sky, or system, is asking of the individual over a period of time, we must take into consideration all the planets' movements. Each planet will repeat its transit of the whole sky in a certain number of years. Saturn will spend about two and a half years in each sign, completing the sign circuit in 29.5 years. Jupiter will spend about a year in each sign, completing its circuit of the whole sky, or the birth chart circle of houses, in 12 years. Mars will spend about two months in each sign, completing its circuit in about 2 years. Mercury, Venus and Sun will activate the houses of the chart yearly. Thus, their effect will seem less dramatic because it will happen so frequently and one finally becomes used to it. But the slower-moving planets activate the signs and houses for those longer periods noted and their influence is felt strongly.

Because of this, we will, in the overall transit view, ignore the planets Venus and Mercury, and the Sun and Moon, because these energy-centers repeat their activations on a yearly or monthly basis and one becomes so used to them that he relegates their effects to relatively minor matters. It is the energy-centers that repeat their cycles every 2 years, every 12 years, every 30 years and every 84 years that must be given first consideration because their impact is less frequent and longer-lasting and some people seem never to become adjusted to them.

When we consider what these transits CAN mean, what they SHOULD mean and what they USUALLY PRODUCE--because people are not prepared for them and what coincides with them--we have to set some orders of importance.

1. The transit of a planet moving in the sky to a planet in the birth chart holds meaning WITHIN the meaning of the house transit. It has, in addition, an effect on the activities of the house, or houses, RULED by the transitting and birth planets as well as the activities we see in the house through which it's moving.

2. The transit of a HOUSE holds meaning WITHIN the greater, longer-lasting meaning of the QUADRANT TRANSIT. This is to say that we are localizing the effect of a growth pattern (the quadrant meaning which holds true for all three of the quadrant's houses at the same time) when we confine the transit meaning to any one house, or field of activity. We must always consider that house activity WITHIN the overall growth potential of which the house is only one of three phases of quadrant growth potential.

3. The quadrant, house and planet transits by moving energy-centers have the greatest effect in an individual's life.

4. The transit of a sign is having an effect on that substance in ALL human beings, and even the institutions they set up that coincide with the nature of the signs. There is a sign transit effect for the individual but it is often within a general social pattern.

what a transit is

When we start to interpret the transits one by one, we must remember that not only is a transit having an effect on this particular life but so are all the transits somewhere in the life, at the same time. The transits of the planets ruling the sign in which the Sun is placed at birth and ruling the sign on the Ascendant will have marked effects in most lives, but all of the transits are having some kind of effect.

Many people feel most personally the transit of a birth planet rather than the effect of the transit of a birth chart house. But it is really the quadrant transits that shape the life from outside, whether the individual is aware of it or not, because that kind of transit is throwing energy at THE VERY SPACE HE OCCUPIES IN RELATION TO THE WHOLENESS OF THE SYSTEM. He may not recognize this or really see it, because it is most visible from outside his inner perspective. He may feel more strongly the transit of a birth planet because such a transit means that SOME PART OF HIM INSIDE is being activated by what's going on outside. But the quadrants are parts of his developing awareness that mark his record in the world and they are being strongly affected. We could make the comparison of a storm arriving. The person may hear it outside the house, but not be affected strongly by it until a gust of wind opens the door and lets the fury of it inside to him. The walls of the house are somewhat like the quadrants and houses of the chart. People outside see them. The person inside is more aware of the birth planets that represent energy-centers of his personality because he is always involved in them; they are part of him and not so visible from outside.

As I consider the transits, one by one, I start with those of the planet Saturn because although we MAY decide to "transform ourselves" (Uranus' urging), "make contact with a greater life role through a rebirth of consciousness" (Neptune's urging by transit) and "initiate ourselves into a greater life role through a rebirth of consciousness" (Pluto's urging by transit), our present world does not teach us to do this or even encourage us in it. But it DOES force us to DEFINE ourselves, to identify ourselves as individuals separate from all other individuals in our personal distinctions whether we like it or not. We all have a name and number in government files. We are forced by living in society to EXPAND our realm of personal influence and ACT or INITIATE things or we do not long survive (these activities are what come from Jupiter and Mars transits).

I consider secondary the transits of the planets Pluto, Neptune and Uranus, in most people's lives, because they are only positive key forces in the lives of persons trying to become INDIVIDUALS BEYOND THE TYPICAL CULTURAL TYPE.

Because response to Pluto, Neptune and Uranus transits is a choice for the majority (especially positive response), does not mean that cultural type individuals are not affected by them. They are, but they try to ignore it. When they do so, they generally place themselves in a negative response pattern (and because these transits last so long in one division of activities, such people often justify what happens in coincidence with them as "fateful accidents" that don't fit normal patterns but which they have managed to "endure"). In this case, for such people, Uranus' transits often produce UNEXPECTED CHANGE, and resultant chaos, rather than transformation. Neptune's transits often produce CONFUSION and what is considered a period of deception, rather than "making contact with a greater world of perception." Pluto's transits can produce UPHEAVAL, COERCION AND COMPULSIVE UPSETS, sometimes even "forced transformations," rather than "an initiation of oneself into a greater life role through a rebirth of consciousness."

It could be otherwise.

There are many textbooks describing WHAT HAS HAPPENED to people as the result of the planetary transits. They are also full of dire assumptions--the main one being that WHAT HAPPENED is BOUND TO HAPPEN AGAIN. The main flaw in this idea is that nothing actually HAPPENED. The individuals whose plights they are considering, or recording, simply RESPONDED IN A CERTAIN MANNER to a set of circumstances to which there COULD have been a choice of response if they had understood themselves and their placement in the scheme of the whole and its constant unfoldment of itself THROUGH them. The system simply throws out the energy. It doesn't tell you precisely how to respond to it. It tells you when the energy is coming, but not what you will do with it. That's your choice.

Astrologers who approach transits with fear are themselves fools.

There is nothing to fear but fear itself and the ignorance it produces.

"Transits" that have coincided with accidents and even deaths have had their PURPOSES, even in the lives they most drastically affected. If we can ever come to believe that something in us lives beyond this petty perception of time and space, we will KNOW that death is but a state of transformation and ACCIDENTS, as we call them, but which could probably be better called a DYNAMIC RESPONSE TO ENERGIES AROUSING US, are often steps into periods of growth that could have happened in no other way. I am not saying we should run toward death or accidents, but I AM saying that they both have their purposes.

Someone always says to me, "But shouldn't I be aware of the possibility of death or an accident?" And I must answer, "You should be aware of the possibility of growth through the death of an old condition--the body does not have to go with it; and you should be aware of the possibility of growth through a dynamic challenge to your structured patterns--an accident does not have to be PHYSICAL and it is often all that will shake you out of a pattern that is outmoded."

There are DEATHS OF STRUCTURED CONSCIOUS STATES always in every life. There are DYNAMIC CHALLENGES TO OUTMODED PATTERNS in many lives, especially those structured for it at birth. These do not have to be responded to negatively and they do not have to result in the death of the body.

The planets' movements are trying to tell us how to respond to what the wholeness of the system is now calling appropriate for EVERYONE, but specifically for the individual in the manner in which the movement affects his own individuality.

An ASTROLOGER cannot tell a person WHAT WILL HAPPEN IN ADVANCE. In fact, he has a responsibility not to do so. He will be psychically living that person's life for him. A divine intervention can present the future in graphic detail but an astrological birth chart cannot. It is like a road map to the territory ahead. It will show you the turns in the road, and it may even warn you of the climate. But YOU will have to make the trip. And you can't KNOW what YOU WILL EXPERIENCE until you do. And that, after all, is why you're going.

Many people will travel the same territory. Some will have mishaps and mechanical breakdowns. Others will sail right through, enjoying every moment. The reason for the difference, most likely, is the preparation of the traveler and the ATTITUDE he takes toward using his will and intelligence rather than submitting himself entirely to environment's pitfalls.

We will consider the planetary transits in this manner.

1. The meaning of a planet transitting in a "sign"--psychologically in the individual and in the mass in mankind.

2. The meaning of a planet's transit or activation of a quadrant in the individual's birth chart.

3. The meaning of a planet's transit or activation of a house or field of activities in the individual's birth chart.

4. The meaning of a planet's transitting "aspect" to its own place and the place of all other planets in the individual's birth chart.

Saturn is saying to the individual that the time has come for him to DEFINE himself in the quadrant, field and energy-center it is affecting. That means he must "face reality" in these matters, the reality that he is an individual separate from other individuals and his defining himself in these matters is making that even more so. It is saying that one can define himself through "patient effort," through an ability to "isolate himself" sometimes, through an ability to "overcome obstacles" at others, but, in all ways, to become "more profound, more formed and steady" in his activities in whatever Saturn is trying to get him to define, in his growing potential (the quadrant transit), in his fields of activity (the house transit) and in his own personality functions or energy-centers (the planet transits, if there are any).

saturn in the signs

Saturn traveling in a sign of the Zodiac is showing where a substance of human nature--or what we could call a human "attitude"--is going to be curbed, disciplined and made to accept boundaries of operation because activities involving that substance are now meant to manifest in some defined form. The world outside one is asking for this to happen. At least it seems that way. And the reason is that at some time previous to this transit (or maybe coincident with it) the planet Saturn, by transit, passed over the conscious, or unconscious, part of the psyche which "governs" this human substance or attitude and set in motion a process of renewal that can now manifest, here, in this division of life where the sign Saturn is at the moment transitting.

Saturn has, at some time (either during this life if one is past the age of 30, or before it, if he is still very young), made a conjunction with that natal planet that "rules" the sign it is now transitting. What happened at the time of that conjunction--wherever it occurred in the birth chart or the individual's personal makeup--is trying to come to fruition NOW in this part of his life activities. In other words, something INSIDE him (some part of his personality, conscious or unconscious--represented by the planet that "rules" this sign) previously went through a process of definition and now the results of that process are ready to come to life IN ACTIVITIES here in the sign quality, the human substance, or the life activity attitude, represented by THIS sign Saturn is transitting. If we look at the "aspect" Saturn is now making to that natal planet, we can see the "ease" (soft aspect) or "difficulty" or "challenge" (hard aspect) that a definition of activities here will call up for the individual. The "purpose" of this ease or difficulty can be seen in the meaning of the "phase" of cycle Saturn is making with that natal planet by its transit now (and in this case we must reverse the usual process of seeing the cycle, now looking at Saturn as the moving, or faster, factor and the natal planet as the reference point--no matter how much faster or slower by transit that natal planet is in the sky--because the natal planet is NOT MOVING).

There are always two ways of looking at Saturn transits. If the individual understands himself and is trying to unfold his own unique potential, then Saturn, by transit, merely represents a TIMING PROCESS. If he does not understand himself and, in fact, is trying to gear himself to standards outside himself (that is, he is trying to become some "cultural model or standard"), then Saturn represents what most astrologers have come to attribute to it--hardship, obstacles, the need for patience and endurance, and heavy pressure to accept SOCIETY'S responsibilities. If the first option can be made to operate it is NOT society's responsibilities or standards one must accept, but the defining force inside him that can make HIS REALITY come into manifestation. This WILL require patience, discipline and acceptance of boundaries--but HIS OWN BOUNDARIES within the potential of his own individuality, rather than those of someone else. Few people, I must say, are actually unfolding their own potential. They are, instead, accepting outer standards and models to mould themselves into. But they COULD become aware of their own potential and live it out. It is for such persons that most of the material in these interpretations is set down.

For those individuals, the transit of Saturn through a sign of the Zodiac located in a specific place in their birth chart, indicates that THE TIME HAS COME TO DEFINE THE ACTIVITIES OF THIS AREA AND MANIFEST IN REAL TERMS WHAT BEGAN AT SOME OTHER TIME (when Saturn transitted the "ruler" of this sign--and if we are to say that this process is applying to specific activities in the life, we must consider the ruler of the sign that is on the CUSP of the house which gives us the key to those activities).

FOCUS YOUR IMPULSES (Saturn is transitting Aries--its "aspect" and phase relation to natal Pluto shows how "a need to perceive your individual role in the system and bring it into real manifestation" in these activities is operating). Aries is that part of you that plunges into experience through self-projection in order to gain self-awareness. It is the part of you that is insecure as an individual and must act again and again to prove itself. Saturn's operation here is to make you FOCUS those impulses so that they will produce more lasting results. This part of you is where a spiritual role you unconsciously realize can manifest now in effective activities that will make your role visible in earthly terms, whether society likes it or not. (The "aspect" of natal Saturn to natal Pluto will show what troubles you will have with your role in the eyes of "established" authority.) The Aries part of you operates on instinct. Saturn does not work easily with "instinct," so you may feel heavily disciplined during this transit. Continue to act on impulse, but don't scatter your energy so much. Focus it, discipline it, and try to make contact with the center inside that often COMPELS you to act. Try to understand it; by the time this transit is over, you probably will have one way or another. For what you do in this part of yourself, from now on, will be of benefit not only to yourself, and your personal growth, but to the growth of all humanity.

ECONOMIZE YOUR PRODUCTION (Saturn is transitting Taurus -- Saturn's transit aspect to natal Venus will show how you are going to learn to deepen your personal values while you trim from them what may have become personal indulgences) -- Taurus is the part of you where things set in motion in Aries become rooted, grounded, and slowed down so that they can produce in tangible terms. This is where you put substance, or reality, into your personal projections and self-awareness. There is a need to touch things, feel them, and experience the sensuality of life, in order to realize that the actions set in motion in Aries came into some solid form. The Taurus part of you operates on instinct, also, but Saturn works easily with the side of it that moves slowly, persistently, and productively. There won't be so much "strain" from this transit unless you are truly indulgent here. What is happening to you now is that you are DEFINING AND SHAPING ECONOMICALLY your ability to put reality into your actions.

CURB YOUR RESTLESSNESS (Saturn is transitting Gemini -- Saturn's transit aspect to natal Mercury will show how you are going to put depth into your thought, communications and personal extensions of yourself. It will show how you are learning that depth, rather than speed, of reaction, is now important.) -- Gemini is where you extend yourself vividly into your surroundings in order that you can make the connections that will make possible solid personal foundations. It is the part of you that is restless for new experiences, new ideas, new connections, to classify and assimilate into your own being. It is also instinctive in action and clever as well. This is where you "talk" your way through, where you spread out verbally, mentally and actionally into your surroundings because you are convinced that you put reality into your own self-projection and self-awareness. This part of you is restless. The energy that Saturn throws out does not combine well with restlessness. One thing that will happen during this transit is that you will probably learn so deeply that you will never forget any information you acquire. You are making PROFOUND your ability to put reality into your self-projection and move it out into your surroundings.

FOCUS YOUR RESPONSES -- (Saturn is transitting Cancer -- Its transit aspect to the natal Moon will show how you are going to make up now for failures of the past --even in past lives--how you are learning to curb your emotions and discipline your moods.) -- Cancer is the part of you where you set up personal boundaries and make yourself secure before you put all your effort into self-expression. It is the part of your nature that is emotionally responsive to everything around it because it is trying to define its own area of operation. It is the part of you that needs personal security before it allow something that will be born later in Aries to start coming to life deep inside. The Cancer part of you is also instinctive and its urge to set up boundaries goes naturally with Saturn's energy--but its fluctuating nature does not. After projecting, making real and extending yourself out into your immediate surroundings you are now SETTING UP THE BOUNDARIES OF YOUR OWN ACTIVITIES. This transit calls for a discipline of fluctuating emotions more than anything else.

saturn in the signs

le

CURB YOUR EGO -- (Saturn is transitting Leo -- Its transit aspect to the natal Sun shows how you are learning to define, and make real in action, your true, inner purpose in this life.) -- Leo is the part of yourself where you begin to stamp your own individual identity on your surroundings, where you express yourself as an individual and where the generosity of your personal nature (if there is that kind of thing in you) reaches out to touch everything with its own gifts. The Leo part of you is secure in itself but it is insecure in its ability to realize how it fits into situations greater than itself. Leo is an instinctive part of you that is naturally confident--of its own worth. Saturn is an energy-force that respects things only in their value to the whole of the community. It demands a curbing of what we call personal ego. The Leo part of your nature may strain against the Saturn energy as much as the Aries part did. But go on--express yourself, reach out with the light of your own personality here. You only have to realize that YOU MUST DEFINE YOURSELF IN TERMS THAT WILL FIT OTHERS' NEEDS AS WELL AS YOURS.

At this point, Saturn has moved through the signs, or human attitudes, that represent the outspreading of the Day Force, or the individual coming to life for his own sake. The process began in Aries. There something that originated in the field of activities where Pluto was located natally, emerged into self-projection and self-awareness. In Taurus, Saturn's movement defined the emergence of something that originated in the field of activities where natal Venus was placed. This gave substance to the emergence of self-awareness. In Gemini, this self-projection which took on substance began to spread itself out into its surrounding. What emerged in Gemini had its origin in the natal house where Mercury was placed and began when Saturn transitted natal Mercury. Something started in Aries, took root in Taurus and spread out in Gemini... In Cancer it focalized itself and set personal boundaries because of some process that began when Saturn last transitted the natal Moon. Now, here in Leo, after starting, becoming substantial and spreading out, then setting boundaries of operation, this process expressed itself in individual terms. Whatever the expression was, it probably originated in the activities of the natal house of the Sun and began when Saturn transitted that point. Now, it comes to manifestation here. And this is the peak of its personal value. From here on, there is a process of self-adjustment and the ability to manifest things in terms of others, rather than oneself.

vi

CONTROL YOUR ANALYSIS -- (Saturn is transitting Virgo -- Its transitting aspect to natal Mercury shows how you are learning to deepen and control the analysis and reductive thinking powers that will allow you not only to be personally efficient but to begin realizing your worth in terms of others.) -- Virgo is the part of you that analyses the excesses of the Leo part of your nature and tries to arrive at efficient methods of operation so there is not a lot of personal waste. It is the part of you where you can be most self-critical or most self-organized. It is the instinctive part of your nature that always questions until it learns HOW something should operate in order that it MAY economize on waste and excess. It is also the part of yourself that can be so absorbed in the details that it forgets the wholeness into which they fit. Saturn energy is very akin to this part of your nature, except for the personally self-destructive potential in it. If you do not tear yourself apart over details, this transit will probably not be bothersome at all, for YOU WILL ECONOMIZE ON THE METHODS THAT MAKE YOU SELF-SUFFICIENT AS WELL AS POTENTIALLY VALUABLE TO EVERYONE ELSE.

li

CONTROL YOUR DETACHMENT -- (Saturn is transitting Libra -- Its transitting aspect to natal Venus shows how you are learning to deepen your group values and perceive what you care about in the light of your social role rather than your personal satisfactions.) -- Libra is the part of you that weighs everything against standards outside the personal. It is the part of you where you become as aware of others as you are of yourself. It is also the part of you that has the most difficult time making a decision, one way or another, because it is always considering both sides of everything. Saturn's energy is very akin to the social side of Libra but very impatient with its tendency to waver in indecision. What will happen under this transit is that you will learn to define your social values--and the values you place on relationship with another person. But you will have to learn that complete detachment is sometimes a form of escape from commitment. You will learn that social values are important BUT THEY WERE MADE FOR THE INDIVIDUAL.

DISCIPLINE YOUR PASSIONS -- (Saturn is transitting Scorpio. -- Its transitting aspect to natal Mars shows how you are learning to control your drives, spiritualize your urges for power and discipline your energies.) --Scorpio is the part of you where you try to make substantial the awareness of what is not yourself in your life. It's the part of you that has an instinct for the management of power and the resources of groups of people or the other person in your life. In a deeper sense, it is the part of your nature where you can focus the energy of greater powers in yourself outward into life. Scorpio is where the "battleground of desire" lies within you--it contains enormous energy for construction or destruction. It requires the passion to focus it and it can lead to the passion to misuse it. Saturn's energy is very much akin to the Scorpio attitude, except that Saturn's energy is ALREADY a disciplined kind. In Scorpio one learns to CONSCIOUSLY use power, as in Taurus one does it instinctively and, in Capricorn, one does it with discipline. What you learn while Saturn transits this area of your makeup is that POWER THAT IS LASTING IS ALWAYS DISCIPLINED. The descents into the darkness to find it are always necessary but they are never engaged in for the mere novelty of it.

FOCUS YOUR THOUGHTS -- (Saturn is transitting Sagittarius. -- Saturn's transitting aspect to natal Jupiter indicates how you are learning to curb excesses and zeals. It shows how you are learning how not to scatter your energies and outward movements but to expand your realms of effectiveness and influence realistically.) -- Sagittarius is the part of you that wants to move out from other-awareness and the power gained from union with others and make the connections that will build more than a group; that will pave the way for a society. It is also the part of you that searches for truth beyond the obvious truths of daily living and personal experience. It is the part of your nature that wants to assimilate large ideas and spread itself ever outward toward adventure and new experience that is NOT part of the daily routine. Saturn's energy is not akin to this outward-spreading and so the transit of this part of your makeup is often painful to it. Saturn's urge is to contain, to set boundaries and the Sagittarius part of you is contemptuous of boundaries. What you learn while Saturn transits this area of your makeup is that your excesses and zeals must be curbed in order that your EXPANSIONS ARE NOT MERE DAYDREAMS BUT THAT THEY BECOME REALITIES that can be used in building your social foundations.

MAKE YOUR ROLE PROFOUND -- (Saturn is transitting Capricorn. --Saturn's transitting aspect to its natal place shows not only how you are learning to see the other side of ambition and social power but what stage a former identity--that you took on spontaneously when Saturn last transitted its natal place--has reached in growth or need for realignment. This is one of the most important of all Saturn aspects by transit. It shows "where you are" in leaving an impression on your world as an individual. It also shows how you are being asked to let something new come to life within your rigid, society-defined sense of "personal boundaries" and "personal worth to the community.") -- Capricorn is the part of you where you reach the peak of ambition and identify yourself as a part of the community in whatever role you have decided to take in it. It is the place in your makeup where traditional roles tend to crystallize themselves in your life. It is the place where you are most austere, cautious and remote to the "personal" aspects of a human life. You can do one of two things in the Capricorn part of your nature. You can find your role within the established lines of thinking or you can search out, inside them, what it is in them that needs to be born, or reborn, in order to transform their no-longer-needed rigidity and authority. It is in this part of your nature that you follow Caesar or Christ. It is either the most "establishment-oriented" part of your nature, or the most austerely spiritual. Saturn's energy is what MAKES Capricorn possible. The planet, in the sky, represents the boundaries of the visible Solar System. One side of it looks back to the king of the system--the Sun, the great autocrat of the conscious world. The other side of it is turned toward the Galaxy--toward the unconscious perceptions that can transform and renew the conscious world. When Saturn transits this part of your nature you learn to WORSHIP THE ESTABLISHED ORDER OF THINGS OR TURN YOUR EYES TO THOSE POWERS WHICH CAN DESTROY ITS STRUCTURE AND RENEW ITS SPIRIT. In other words, when Saturn transits this part of you, as a result of what it set up when it transitted its own natal place, it can allow you, in this part of your makeup, to be open to the transforming powers of Uranus, Neptune and Pluto; or turn your back on them in profound and spirit-shrinking fear.

**saturn
in
the
signs**

aq

pi

FOCUS YOUR URGE FOR REFORM -- (Saturn is transitting Aquarius. -- Its transitting aspect to natal Uranus shows how you are learning to bring originality and innovation into concrete form. It shows how you are curbing the urge to rebel for rebellion's sake and make your innovations fit the world's needs.) --In the Aquarius part of your nature you have the opportunity to express through yourself ideas that are not yourself but are common to the benefit of anyone and everyone. In the Aquarius part of yourself you have the ability to reflect into your surroundings the enormous power of Man, and not the single ego. In this part of your nature you are most insecure as an individual, but absolutely certain of your right to represent the freedom of the individual within the group. In this part of yourself you will have to gain security as an individual by MANAGING THE POWER OF THE GROUP not for your own benefit but for the benefit of everyone. The legend of Aquarius is that he was cupbearer of the Gods; he poured the waters of life down to any of mankind who would accept them. What he was pouring was the power of the One that encompasses All down to anyone who would accept it. It was electrifying, spirit-reforming power. When Saturn transits this part of your nature, it has actually made possible a defiance of its energy. But use that energy, and defy it at the same time (that is, to use the power of focusing and disciplining energy in order to re-order the pattern of its distribution) requires that THE URGE FOR REFORM BE FOCUSED ON WHAT NEEDS TO BE REFORMED. This is a powerful transit and makes or breaks the person who wants to see the world change for the better. The power to change lies in his own hands; he can use or misuse it, for in this part of himself, at this time, he is becoming the manager of a power greater than himself and it CAN overwhelm him.

FOCUS YOUR CONTACTS WITH GREATER WORLDS -- (Saturn is transitting Pisces. --Its transitting aspect to natal Neptune shows how you are learning to bring your perceptions of what is nebulous but ready to take life down into the real world. It shows how you bring imagination into real form. It shows how you take the power of intuition, or contact with the unconscious, and bring it into reality.) The Pisces part of your nature is where you decide to turn your back on established forms (even though you understand them probably better than anyone else here) and move out into a nebulous world where you have nothing to guide you but faith. This is the part of your nature where you have to quit clinging to what is familiar and move toward what has not taken any tangible form. And you have to believe that it will. The Pisces part of your nature is where you will undergo some of the greatest, and most subtle, tests of your life. It is here that you truly must sacrifice ego in order that what is waiting to come to life, in some new form in Aries, can have the faith of the past to bring it to life. You must give yourself up--by clinging to the old as it falters and dies and takes you with it; or stepping out of its dimensions into that world that is just beyond it and focusing its power for a rebirth into the next cycle of activity. Saturn's energy is akin to the spirit of Pisces, but not to the "form" of it. Saturn, the myth-figure, has been called the chronocrater--we could say, "the timer." When he reaches this part of the Zodiac, not only does the ego die but so does all the energy and form that accompanied the Saturn energy-center up to this point. In other words, when Saturn reaches this field of your activities, the WORLDLY side of what it represents (your concept of yourself within society's terms and standards) must now plunge itself into the sea of the unconscious and be initiated into a higher form of concept through Pluto's realm. When Saturn transits Pisces worldly ambition is subtly thwarted or brought to life in a new way. A cycle has ended. In this part of yourself, always, CYCLES OF ACTIVITY AND CONSCIOUSNESS ARE ENDING. They die in the activities of this house and emerge anew in the activities of the Aries house. However it affects you, when Saturn moves in Pisces, something important in your life is dying in form in order that it can re-emerge in an insecure new one in Aries. And the power that has been building in DEFINITION (Saturn's energy-field) since its last transit of Aries is now sinking into the unconscious to come up in a new KIND of definition. That is why it is so important that you now FOCUS YOUR CONTACTS WITH GREATER WORLDS OF PERCEPTION because you will NEED THEIR POWER in what is about to come.

Anyone who wants to understand what is happening to him, through the forces that are acting on him from outside, should understand what he was equipped to have come into definition, at birth, and then understand that this definition has three levels of operation. That is, one must understand that each planet is located in a certain sign, quadrant, house and disposition to the other parts of his nature (in aspect to all the other planets in his personal sky) AT HIS BIRTH -- and this represents POTENTIAL. Each planet moves on, in the sky, after his birth, from the position it held at his birth. It moves on through each sign of the Zodiac, through each house of his birth chart, through each quadrant of the same chart, and through all the possible aspects of a cycle -- both in relation to its own place and in relation to the moving places of all the other planets. The positions at birth ARE HIS POTENTIAL. The positions AFTER BIRTH are steps TO THE REALIZATION OF THAT POTENTIAL.

In other words, let us say, you were born when the planet Saturn was located in Pisces. Your basic potential as an individual, as far as your basic defining power goes in relation to the substance of Pisces in your nature, is that YOU CAN FOCUS THE CONTACTS YOU HAVE WITH GREATER WORLDS. It is natural to you. But after you are born, this will work in three ways. First, for the first 28 to 30 years of your life, it will be an instinctive process that is in you and simply works. And with this ability, for the first 30 years of your life, you are paying your way in society, in some way or another. It may be that your society does not like this ability. Nevertheless, it is operative in you and if they could but see it, it offers you a way of doing that society a service while you are preparing to DEVELOP THE ABILITY IN ANOTHER WAY at about the age of 30. At that time, Saturn, by transit, will return to its own position and say to you, "Begin a new cycle of defining yourself. This time, do it not because of what you are taught, or what you already knew; no, do it now in a way that will make you a self-sufficient individual ready to let a higher individuality (represented in its first nature by the planet Uranus at your birth) come to life IN WHAT YOU HAVE BEEN TAUGHT IN THIS SOCIETY. Uranus, at your birth, may be so disposed that it will rebel against what your Saturn, or defining ability, has already made of you. If it is in a different "sign" of the Zodiac, it will want to operate (that is the higher potential of individuality) in a manner that is different than the individuality allowed by the birth sign position of Saturn. But it will want to operate THROUGH the vehicle you created with that birth Saturn power of definition.

At the age of 30, or before or shortly after, you will have what is called "an identity crisis." You will come to that period when you will have to decide "whether you are going to be yourself or what others have so far expected of you, taught you or made necessary for you to conceive of yourself in order to survive." Now, you are on your own. Society (or a past life's tradition, if you prefer to see it that way) gave you the ability to do what I have already outlined with Saturn in each of the sign positions. What must happen around the age of 30, is that you start using this ability IN A WAY THAT WILL ALLOW YOU TO BECOME AN INDIVIDUAL IN YOUR OWN RIGHT. And if that is to happen, we must consider what the individual inside, waiting to come out around that age, is equipped to do, because of the birth "sign" location of the planet Uranus. That will be covered here in a later section.

At the age of 56 to 60 there will be another return of Saturn to its birth position, by transit, and this will mark a time when you can GO BEYOND THE POTENTIAL OF INDIVIDUAL SELF-EXPRESSION. At that time, if you have gone through the potential of the Uranus birth position, you can then enter the potential of the birth position of NEPTUNE--and make "an actual connection with what lies beyond individuality, what lies beyond reality and what is, in essence, your umbilical cord to a world of greater understanding."

The reason I have mentioned this, at this point, is that Saturn, by transit, will pass over both Uranus and Neptune's birth positions, before you arrive at the age of 30. What will be happening, in groundwork ways at those times, is a defining process of WHAT CAN HAPPEN when Saturn returns to its own position at age 30 (it can lay the groundwork for the potential of the second 30 years of your life when it crosses your birth Uranus position) and when it returns again at age 60 (it can lay the groundwork for the potential of the third part of your life when it crosses your birth Neptune position). In other words, there will probably be strange, almost indecipherable, things happening then that will turn up in later works, or pathways to realization of any kind, in major parts of your life.

growth set by quad-rant

What I am saying, now, in essence, is this: When I come to the point of interpretting the transit of Saturn over natal Uranus and natal Neptune, I will be saying that you should DEFINE YOUR INDIVIDUALITY (transitting S$_a$turn passing over birth Uranus' position) and DEFINE YOUR CONTACTS WITH GREATER WORLDS OF PERCEPTION (when transitting Saturn passes over birth Neptune's position). I will also be saying, as I already have done here, that Saturn's transit of Uranus --the results of what happened then--can emerge into your psyche and your life when it later transits the house bearing the sign Aquarius (and in the activities that house represents and in a manner of ease or difficulty that is represented by transitting Saturn's aspect to natal Uranus when it is making the transit of Aquarius). I will be saying that Saturn's transit of Neptune can later show up in your life and your psyche when it subsequently transits the sign Pisces (and in the activities that house represents and in the manner of ease or difficulty of its transitting aspect to birth Neptune's position at the time of that subsequent transit of Pisces).

Essentially, I am trying to show you that even in the early part of your life, events that develop from Saturn's transit of Uranus will be bringing out, probably unconsciously, what natal Uranus' meaning can spread across the whole second thirty years of your life. Events that develop, even the first time from Saturn's transit of Neptune--but probably much more strongly the second time-- can show on unconscious levels what's likely to color the third part of your life (if we consider Neptune's birth position as potential).

Saturn takes about two and a half years to transit each sign in your birth chart. It gives you that amount of time to feel that forces from outside are asking you to define yourself in those substances of your nature. For instance:

If you were born when Saturn was in Aries, you possess the ability to FOCUS YOUR IMPULSES. In order to get this up to a higher level of meaning, you must go through the process of ECONOMIZING YOUR PRODUCTION (the transit of Taurus), DEEPENING YOUR THINKING (transit of Gemini), FOCUSING YOUR RESPONSES (transit of Cancer), CURBING YOUR EGO (transit of Leo), CONTROLLING YOUR ANALYSIS (transit of Virgo), DEEPENING YOUR AWARENESS (transit of Libra), DISCIPLINING YOUR PASSIONS (transit of Scorpio), FOCUSING YOUR THOUGHTS (transit of Sagittarius), DEEPENING YOUR SOCIAL WORTH (transit of Capricorn), FOCUSING YOUR URGE FOR REFORMS (transit of Aquarius), FOCUSING YOUR CONTACTS WITH GREATER WORLDS (transit of Pisces) in those activities where these things are emphasized AND IN THAT ORDER, in order that when Saturn returns to its place you can once again FOCUS YOUR IMPULSES AT A DIFFERENT LEVEL in order that you can become the individual (natal Uranus' meaning) that was latent inside the vehicle your past lives or your society created (natal Saturn's meaning) FOR ITS INDIVIDUAL OPERATION AFTER THE AGE OF 30.

If you were born with Saturn in another sign of the Zodiac, you will follow the process of getting back to a different level of your natal Saturn's meaning IN THE ORDER OF THE DEFINITIONS THAT FOLLOWS YOUR NATAL SATURN'S BASIC POTENTIAL. Or, if Saturn were in Libra when you were born, you already possess the ability, in some way, to DEEPEN YOUR AWARENESS. The next steps to raising this to a higher level will be to concentrate on DISCIPLINING YOUR PASSIONS, FOCUSING YOUR THOUGHTS, and so on back to the natal position.

You don't have to understand this, but it will show you a great deal about what's been trying to happen in your life. In the order it's been trying to happen. We are all different. Depending on how we were born with a capacity to naturally define ourselves, we will go through this whole order of defining different attitudes in different activities of our lives IN A DIFFERENT ORDER OF EXPRESSION (depending on where Saturn began at birth--for that determines the whole order of identity that goes on inside the individuality).

After we have seen that flow of defining attitudes, we must see to what it applies in our lives.

These attitudes will be developed in the previous order, but WHERE WILL THEY BE WORKING IN THE INDIVIDUAL?

What part of his TRUE INDIVIDUALITY AS AN INDIVIDUAL PERSON OCCUPYING A UNIQUE PLACE IN SPACE will be affected and when?

There is a three-fold order to that, too, and will not necessarily follow this order. And it is much stronger in defining EVENTS.

What I was saying previously about the order of developing attitudes in your basic makeup will not be as striking as what the development of great fields and specific fields of activity in your life will produce, but it will explain some of the things that are going on within those activities.

Everyone follows an order of attitude-development that moves in the order of the "signs" as Saturn passes through them. Everyone also follows an order of activity-development that moves in the order of the quadrants and houses as Saturn moves counterclockwise through THEM.

In both cases, we go through development that CAN move on three levels of expression, if we learn to understand ourselves apart from what we are taught. The first 28 years of development is for the purpose of CREATING A VEHICLE IN WHICH INDIVIDUALITY (Uranus, Neptune and Pluto) CAN OPERATE IN SOCIETY. During this first 28-year period, parents and cultural forces are strong in the shaping of the "structure" (Saturn natally) of this vehicle. In fact, they can have an overwhelming, and even detrimental force upon it if they do not understand the child's real makeup--if they try to view him in terms of what they "want him to be" rather than in terms of "what he potentially is" (which is written in the birth chart).

The second 28 years of development, of both attitudes and activities, is for the purpose of INDIVIDUAL SELF-EXPRESSION (what the total birth chart held as a potential) and the FORM OF IDENTITY can now be structured by the Uranus position AND the Saturn position, because Uranus' meaning will try to lift the Saturn meaning to a higher level of expression, one on terms of "individuality" (Uranus) rather than "cultural identity" (Saturn, in the respect that one's "father" and the "name" he gives one has a tremendous influence upon the "form" he takes in the eyes and minds of others). When Saturn, by transit, returns to the position it held at birth, it is time for this transformation to begin. We could say that one cycle of "structural form" has ended and another has begun. At the time transitting Saturn conjoins its natal position, transitting Uranus makes a first-quarter trine to its natal position, pouring down into the higher-individuality mechanism of the birth chart potential, the "creative power" (trine aspect) of what "an individual transformation" (transitting Uranus) can bring into this life in an "active form to clear away the structures of the past" (the meaning of the first-quarter phase of cyclic energy in which the trine, or 120-degree "aspect," is operating).

So, we could say, at about 30 years of age, one should gear his Saturn nature up to a higher level by attempting to listen to what the Uranus, or individual-izing forces, inside and outside, are trying to say to him.

The ease or difficulty of this process of listening to the Uranian forces can be seen by the "aspects" transitting Uranus is making to all the natal planets-- how this process can work on the level of "transforming one's basic purposes to the individual level, or using the image-making power," (transitting Uranus' aspect and phase to natal Sun, considered within the LATENT Power in the natal Sun-Uranus aspect); "transforming one's ability to bring basic purpose into daily application" (transitting Uranus' aspect and phase to natal Moon, considered within the natural ability shown by the natal Uranus-Moon aspect and phase); "transforming the ability to think or assimilate" (transitting Uranus' aspect to natal Mercury considered within the basic Uranus-Mercury natal phase and aspect); "transforming one's values to the task" (transitting Uranus' aspect to natal Venus considered within the basic Uranus-Venus natal phase and aspect); "transforming one's desires to the task" (transitting Uranus' aspect to natal Mars considered within the basic Uranus-Mars energy potential shown by the natal phase and aspect); "transforming one's ability to expand his realm of influence to the task" (transitting Uranus' aspect to natal Jupiter considered within the basic Uranus-Jupiter phase and aspect at birth); and, most important of all, "the ability to transform one's own developed concept of himself as a cultural individual to the task" (transitting Uranus' aspect to natal Saturn considered WITHIN the birth Uranus-Saturn combination that shows how the INDIVIDUATION PROCESS is likely to act, for the first 30 years, instinctive-ly, and for the second 30 years, knowingly, if it is possible for the individual to know himself and his potential).

All of these are considerations that do not HAVE to be made, but if they are they will very likely show the complete condition in effect at the time of the Saturn return and the "identity crisis" that marks so many lives and which we have NOT been taught, by our society, to expect. We certainly have not been taught how to cope with it. But the answer lies there, in the natal chart, considered in its

**growth
set
by
quad-
rant**

total potential and in the transit pattern which shows the timing of releasing the natal potential. And when I say that, I mean the timing THAT IS PROVIDED BY FORCES OUTSIDE ONESELF. There is another kind of timing, shown by the secondary progressions, and this is important, too. But it is a thing that is PROVIDED FROM INSIDE BY THE INTELLIGENCE THAT IS TRYING TO BRING POTENTIAL TO LIFE IRRESPECTIVE OF CONDITIONS OF THE ENVIRONMENT.

What we are looking at, in transits, IS THE CONDITION OF THE ENVIRONMENT IN RELATION TO THIS INDIVIDUAL POTENTIAL we are considering.

There is still another kind of timing, being released from inside, or from what we might call "fate" or the forces of "genetic patterning and cultural training." This timing is seen in the solar arc directions.

The transits, for most people, however, are the most spectacular revealers of the life's motion and this is probably because we are taught to consider what is outside us more important than what is inside. When that teaching changes, the "transits" may have much less effect on an individual life than they do now.

For now, however, they are the major consideration for most people.

And because they are, it is extremely difficult for most people to respond to the third level of activity represented by the Saturn transits that begin to repeat after the age of 56-60.

This latter age is when Saturn makes its second return. It, too, represents an "identity crisis." But this time, the crisis should not be so centered around breaking away from what was outside (the cultural Saturn forces) to what was inside individually (the Uranus forces in a person and in the sky); no, this time, it should be a movement toward a "greater unfolding" of what was inside. This time, it should be a movement toward Neptunian forces. While Uranus represents unique individual potential, Neptune represents one's "real connection with what is greater even than individuality" and that is the realization that even though one is an individual he belongs to a spiritual unit. We could say it is the realization that though he has performed an individual task in life (or could have, between the ages of 30 and 60), there comes a time when he needs to move out of the exclusiveness of that individualism and relate to what it CAME OUT OF. What it came out of is the true power of the personal and collective unconscious, or what we could call "a man's ability to relate to the powers in the universe that give him life, that give him the spirit that moves in the body."

Neptune takes about twice as long as Uranus to transit the Zodiac, so when Uranus is making its second trine to its natal place (about the age of 56), Neptune is making its first trine, while Saturn, by transit, is again making a conjunction with its own place. The Neptune trine represents a "creative downpouring" (120-degree aspect, by transit) of "spiritual power and realization of oneself within the greater whole" (Neptune used at its higher level) "in an active way that will tear away the props of the past and lead one toward a new kind of realization of himself" (the first-quarter phase meaning of energy flowing through Neptune). At the same time, the Uranus trine, in its second manifestation, occurs within the "disseminating phase" which represents "the ability to convey, consciously to his surroundings, what a man has learned to believe through experience" and again this is a "creative flow" (120-degree aspect) of power. By the time the Neptune trine is complete, Uranus, at about age 63, will move into a square with its natal position. This is the "last quarter square," which means there will be a release of power that "challenges" (90-degree aspect) the individual to "move away from his previous individual identity and prepare for a rebirth of purpose inside" (the meaning of the last-quarter phase when related to Uranus power).

What I have just been talking about could be summed up as being a consideration of the CYCLES OF POSITION operating, because of transits, in a person's life pattern. The correlation of the position cycles, what you might call their "choreography" of action, will happen in ALL LIVES, on this schedule, which moves according to AGE OF A PERSON.

But there is another group of cycles of position that has nothing to do with age. It is entirely geared to the individual's birth time and birth place. And it is the cycle of positions each transitting planet makes to the birth chart AXIS and its subsidiary field of "house" or "fields of activity."

This is seen--considering Saturn first, again--in the 29.5 year movement of Saturn, by transit, through that house structure.

It, too, will be repeated three times, if one lives beyond 84.

TRUE INDIVIDUAL CIRCUMSTANCES OF YOUR LIFE (shaped by the movement of forces outside yourself) can only be known by knowing your birth time and birth place. And that is only appropriate, for your "unique individuality" (shown by the sign and degree rising, or the Ascendant, at your birth) can only be found in that way. Your "cultural identity" (natal Saturn), your "transformed cultural identity (natal Saturn after it has been conjoined by transitting Saturn) and your "spiritualized cultural identity" (Saturn after it has been conjoined the second time by transitting Saturn) HAVE TO WORK WITHIN THIS UNIQUE INDIVI- DUALITY. As a matter of fact, your "cultural identity" (natal Saturn), can only act strongly in the field of activities (the house placement) it attains BECAUSE OF YOUR UNIQUE INDIVIDUALITY (its placement in the birth sky because of the circle of "houses" drawn off FROM the Ascendant and Midheaven of a chart).

Let's consider that individuality and the axis of space it places you in on this earth.

That axis also becomes a position to which transitting Saturn makes cyclic movements and it is most effective in most people's lives because it RELATES DIRECTLY TO THE UNFOLDING OF EVENTS AND ACTIVITIES IN THEIR LIVES.

Saturn, and all the other transitting planets, in the nature of the power they are releasing into the environment, set up a timing schedule for events and activities GEARED TO THE CIRCLE OF HOUSES in the birth chart. Saturn's is about a 30-year cycle and thus it relates strongly to a number of other timing cycles going on in the individual (the Saturn return takes about 30 years, the Uranus trine takes about 30 years, the Neptune trine takes a double 30 years, the progressed Moon moves around the chart in close to 30 years, the progressed New and Full Moon cycle works on a 30-year basis and many of the solar arc directions (because natal planets are often located one "sign" or 30 degrees apart) take about 30 years).

So the cycle of positions of Saturn is very noticeable (partly, too, because human beings physically go through major changes in 30-year cycles) even though some of the other, less considered, cycles in astrology are probably producing many of the things that transit-oriented astrologers are attributing to Saturn cycles.

Because of your birth time and place, your individual life has been given a TIMING SCHEDULE for the unfolding of OVERALL REALIZATIONS and ACTIVI- TIES WITHIN THEM. I've already shown that your birth year (Saturn is located in "signs" on about a two and a half year basis) gives you an order and flow, in timing, of unfolding attitudes and, in the case of Saturn, of defining them. Now, I am saying that this order of attitude-definition TAKES PLACE WITHIN the timing schedule of individual realization and individual activity (in other words the "signs" are located "in" the HOUSE structure of the chart).

That pattern of individual realization and activities is sectioned off into FOUR MAJOR DIVISIONS (four major development patterns) and TWELVE MINOR ONES (each major one containing three minor ones).

Your birth chart has four quadrants and twelve houses, with three houses lying within each quadrant. The effect of a transitting planet on activity development is subsidiary to the effect of a transitting planet upon REALIZATION DEVELOP- MENT (the transits through the quadrants). The development of activities (the transits through the houses) happen within the development of individual realizations.

The first quadrant runs from the Ascendant of the birth chart to its fourth house cusp. It contains the first, second and third houses of the chart. It represents, on the quadrant level, THE INDIVIDUAL REALIZATION OF A GROWTH IN ESSENTIAL BEING. This is accomplished, as Saturn moves through it, by "defining self-awareness and self-projection" (first house) for a growth in essential being (first quadrant); "defining the substance of self-awareness and self-projection" (second house) for a growth in essential being; and "defining the extension of the substance of your self-awareness and self-projection" (third house) for a

ZI

growth set by quad- rant

growth in essential being (first quadrant). The sign, at the beginning of this quadrant, shows (by Saturn's transit-meaning in that sign) the kind of attitude that is being redefined for a growth in essential being. The signs on the cusps of each of the houses in this quadrant show the attitudes that are being redefined (by Saturn's transit through them) in the subsidiary processes of defining self-awareness and self-projection (sign on first house); defining the substance of both those (sign on second house) and defining the extension of this substantial self-awareness out into the surroundings of its environment (sign on third house). If there are any planets, located at birth, in these houses and this quadrant, the DEFINITION OF <u>THOSE PARTS OF THE PERSONALITY AND WHAT THEY REPRESENT will be major developments</u> in this process of growth in essential being.

Grant Lewi, one of the few mid-Twentieth Century astrologers to realize the signi-fance of the transits of outer planets through the quadrants of the chart, defined this first quadrant as a period of "obscurity" in his book, "Astrology for the Mil-lions." While that definition holds true for many people, because they put "success according to outside standards" ahead of "realizing oneself despite outside standards," it will not hold true for anyone who heeds the voice within or who heeds the true potential of himself IN THE SOLAR SYSTEM and not in any particular society's eyes. Such a person may find obscurity in the eyes of others but he will not necessarily find it in the light of his own personal development within the greater potential he can discover that lies within him. Dane Rudhyar, who called this transit quadrant the one of "growth in essential being" geared his astrology almost entirely to the individual trying to discover himself and his unique potential, and not society's standard of what he should be. Society, in general, before the 1970's especially, has refused to recognize the Solar System's image inside a man and has, in doing this, refused to recognize an individual's true potential, or destiny. While I have often taught what Lewi explained, I have always realized that I was teaching very "cultural-success"-oriented interpretations of what was <u>essentially a TRUE REALIZATION ABOUT THE STRUCTURE OF THE INDIVIDUAL"S RELATION TO THE SPACE AROUND HIM.</u> Because the structure was true does not necessarily mean that one man's interpretation of its MEANING would hold true forever. For those people, born and educated to "cultural-success" symbols, who could not understand their individuality in terms of whole systems and not specific cultural systems, Lewi's interpretations hold amazingly true. But anyone who goes outside those "culture-success" orientations will find that OTHER THINGS ARE POSSIBLE. Since Lewi's interpretations are already well-written for the people who think in that manner, I will not be redundant and simply repeat them in new words. The interpretations, that you will find here, will be geared to the man who can believe he is an individual in rapport with the Solar System first of all and then, in subsidiary terms, with all of the cultural structures in which he exists IN that Solar System. This must be explained before considering the Second Quadrant because Lewi called it an "emergence" cycle, meaning an "emergence from obscurity" in social terms. But Rudhyar has called it a cycle of "growth in human capacity" as the result of a "growth in essential being." In both respects, in social standards and in individual standards, it IS an "emergence." But while I would use those terms of Lewi's that strike true in all ways (and he was a master of the striking, and quintessential phrase), I cannot accept, for the individual, the social-success syndrome in which they are couched. This will be true, also, when I come to interpretting the transits of the planets over the birth planetary positions. While Lewi's terms often hold true, in a specific case, the moral vision that focuses them into those words, does not, necessarily. And this must be understood because Lewi was one of the truly great pioneers of bringing astrology to the level where ANY MAN could make use of it

Z2

The second quadrant contains all the Zodiacal space from the fourth house cusp to the cusp of the seventh. It thus contains the fourth, fifth and sixth houses. <u>It is the experience growth realm of A GROWTH IN HUMAN CAPACITY</u>, containing

the experiences of "focalizing self-awareness and self-projection" (fourth house), "raising it to self-expression" (fifth house) and "making the self-adjustments that are necessary to becoming aware of what lies outside self-involvement" (sixth house). When Saturn transits this quadrant circumstances call for a DEFINITION OF GROWTH IN HUMAN CAPACITY through the ability to DEFINE THE FOCALIZATION OF YOUR ACTIVITIES (fourth house), DEFINE YOUR SELF-EXPRESSION (fifth house) and DEFINE YOUR ABILITY TO ADJUST TO WHAT LIES BEYOND SELF-INVOLVEMENT. The sign on the fourth house cusp (and its degree meaning holds a great deal that will amplify this) shows how an attitude (the sign on the cusp) will go through definition in order to achieve a definition of focalization of self-awareness. But it shows, in even more major terms, what attitude will be defined in order that you can, throughout this quadrant, define your growth in human capacity. The sign on the fifth house cusp shows an attitude that will be defined in order that you can define your self-expression, and the sign on the sixth house cusp shows an attitude that will be defined (as I have already explained this under the Saturn "sign" transits) in order that you can define the self-adjustments necessary to becoming aware of what is outside self-involvement. If there are any planets, at birth, located in this quadrant, Saturn's transit of them will show parts of the personality that will undergo definition (interpretted later under Saturn "planet" transits) in the process of defining your growth in human capacity and the subsidiary activities (self-focalization, self-expression and self-adjustment) that make it possible.

The third quadrant runs from the cusp of the seventh house to the cusp of the tenth house, encompassing the seventh, eighth and ninth houses, or fields of experience of the birth chart. It is the realm of GROWTH IN HUMAN FUNCTION-ING which includes "awareness of others" (7th house); "the substance of awareness of others" (8th house); and "an extension of other-awareness and the substance of it into the social surroundings" (9th house). When Saturn transits this quadrant of the birth chart, you will learn to DEFINE YOUR GROWTH IN HUMAN FUNCTION-ING by "defining your awareness of others" (7th house); "defining the substance of your awareness of others" (8th house); and "defining your extension into the social surroundings the substance of your awareness of others" (9th house). The sign on the seventh house cusp shows the attitude you will define in order to go through a growth in human functioning (the transit of the quadrant) and then in order to define your awareness of others in your life (transit of the 7th by Saturn); in order to define the substance of your awareness of others you will develop and define the attitude represented by the sign on the eighth house; and in order to define your extension into the social surroundings of your awareness of others you will go through the development of the attitude signified by the sign on the cusp of the ninth house. If there are any planets located in this quadrant, at birth, the parts of the personality they represent will go through a definition process in order to attain this GROWTH IN HUMAN FUNCTIONING. (Grant Lewi called this the quadrant of "opportunity," meaning that Saturn's transit was opening up "social opportunity" for the individual after his previous "obscurity"--Saturn's transit of the first quadrant--and "emergence from obscurity," or Saturn's transit of the second quadrant.)

The fourth quadrant runs from the cusp of the tenth house to the cusp of the first, encompassing the 10th, 11th and 12th fields of activity. It represents GROWTH IN INFLUENCE as the result of the previous growths "in essential being," "in human capacity" and in "human functioning." When Saturn transits this quadrant of the birth chart, one learns to "focalize his image among others, or his foundations in society" (10th house); to "define his expression through others" (11th house); and to "define the social or self-adjustments he must make in order to begin a new cycle of self-development at another level" (12th house). This last quadrant transit prepares him for a "rebirth in the definition of self-awareness and self-projection" (the next transit of Saturn through the first quadrant and then on through the others). The sign on the 10th house shows the attitude he needs to define in order to GROW IN INFLUENCE. It also shows the attitude he needs to

growth set by quad- rant

focalize or make deeper in order to "focalize his image among others." The sign on the 11th house shows the attitude that will be defined while he "defines his be defined as he "defines the social- or self-adjustments he must make in order to begin a new cycle of self-development at another level." If there are any planets in this quadrant, at birth, those parts of the personality will also undergo definition in order to attain growth in influence.

(To understand these quadrants, and what circumstances--or the energy-flows in the sky--are trying to release in the individual through them, is to get a grasp on the main development patterns of the life. In other words, when you look at your birth chart, and locate by an ephemeris where the planet Saturn is now transitting, you ought to be able to see immediately what kind of growth pattern circumstances has already activated in you, what kind of growth pattern is now in effect, and what kind of growth pattern is immediately ahead. Once you have learned to do this, you can look at any birth chart, and see the rhythms of development that circumstances are going to unfold across the life.

(From the moment it crosses the Ascendant, by transit, Saturn is unfolding a process of definition that operates on all levels--in attitudes because of its movement through the signs, in experience because of its movement in the quadrants, and in activities because of its movement in the houses, and, within this, in parts of the personality because of its transit to them. If you can grasp this pattern quickly, by seeing in your mind what its previous transits have meant, what its current transit is calling forth and what its future transits are going to unfold ahead, you are seeing one of the great worldly processes that goes on in any individual.

(Grant Lewi's book, "Astrology for the Millions," was strikingly impressive and made a great impression on the astrology-conscious world because he did this simply and in the words and morals of his time and showed others how to do it in their own minds. Your grasp of the unfolding of potential through circumstances can be just as impressive but more profound.

(Remember that you are seeing, in your mind, a process that has always been working because always has energy been   released in the sky--on the schedule of the transitting planets. And always will it be as long as the order of the Solar System continues on schedule. Men are moved, especially when they are not even aware of them, by large, cyclic flows of energy that are received by everyone. They cannot really avoid them, but must do something with them one way or another because they are standing in their tides. And that is just what we are seeing through the transits--the tides of energy that surround an individual. He must move through them, either with them or against them. There are other tides moving within him--the progressions and the solar arc directions--but these are moving EVERYONE AT THE SAME TIME, though in different specific ways because they were structured differently, by birth time and place, to receive that energy into their own individual structures.

(Once we have grasped the quadrant meanings, we can always tell, overall, what the thing the person is experiencing most closely now (the transit of a planet, putting pressure on him to define a part of his personality; and the transit of a house, putting pressure on him to define a field of his activities) is leading to. We can see what it developed out of, where it stands now, and where it is headed. Through understanding the quadrants, in other words, we get a frame of reference for three great cycles approximately 30-years in length in his life. The first one, because of transitting Saturn's movement, is the development of A VEHICLE FOR INDIVIDUAL SELF-EXPRESSION. This lasts, in attitudes, for 29.5 years, starts with development of the attitude (sign) in which Saturn is located at birth and unfolds in the order of those that follow. The HOUSE POSITION of Saturn at birth shows WHAT KIND OF GROWTH IN EXPERIENCE AND IN ACTIVITY is beginning at birth, and through WHAT ACTIVITIES AND EXPERIENCE this will progress. And you will see, immediately, that because people have Saturn located at different places in their birth charts, some of them will begin life with a "growth in essential being" to create this vehicle (Saturn in the first quadrant at birth); some of them will begin with a "growth in human capacity" to create this vehicle (Saturn in the second quadrant at birth); some of them will begin with

(Saturn will return to its own place, for a rebirth of identity, at age 30, no matter WHAT quadrant is being activated at that time. So all people will not undergo "a growth in essential being" when they begin to "redefine their cultural selves" at the age of 30. Some will be undergoing a "growth in human capacity" at that time; others will be undergoing a "growth in human functioning" and still others will be undergoing a "growth in influence." The KIND of growth in experience is most important to that individual in COPING with his identity crisis at about age 30, in order to create a higher definition of his cultural self in which Uranus forces can operate to make him an individual. We can see the MAJOR CHARACTER of different peoples' lives by comparing these things. We can also see ages when these things will come into being for different people (even though they all undergo SOME KIND of "identity crisis" around 30--we just see where it is happening in experience of individual growth (quadrant) and individual activities (house) and in the attitudes applying to them (sign) or in any personality function located in them (planet) by locating the QUADRANT the Saturn return occurs in). We can see the ages by realizing that the "amount of sign" in each quadrant represents a TIME PERIOD based upon Saturn's movement of about two and a half years through each sign. You should become aware--and this is easier to see on a continental chart form than it is on the American form where the houses LOOK equal in "sign" size but actually are not--that in northern hemisphere births, in particular, some quadrants contain MORE DEGREES OF SIGN THAN OTHERS and therefore it takes Saturn longer to move through them, or any other planet longer to move through them. You should always note, too, that it will take any planet the same amount of time to travel through the quadrant opposite as it will to travel through the one we are considering. This is so because there are always the SAME number of degrees in the upper half of the chart as there are in the bottom, and the same number of degrees in the left hand side of the chart as the right hand side; BUT OFTEN THE QUADRANTS THAT LIE SIDE BY SIDE ON THE CIRCLE ARE LARGER OR SMALLER IN SIZE BY NUMBER OF DEGREES OF 'SIGN' THEY CONTAIN. In other words, some individuals will have a long period of growth in essential being while their growth in human capacity is short. Other individuals will experience just the opposite. And this, too, in consideration of that individual, in relation to others, is important if you are to understand what he is going through, and will go through, in life, because of the energy that is whirling around him from outside and through which he must make his way to self-fulfillment.)

NOTE: Throughout this book, in the margins, the reader will find letter and number symbols placed next to the conventional astrological symbols. The reading of these symbols is very simple. The capital letter symbols represent planets. Each planet is represented by capitalizing the first two letters of its name in English (there is one exception, since the system originated in Germany--that is the Sun which is represented by SO because Sonne is the word in German). Each sign of the Zodiac is represented by using the first two letters of its symbol spelled out--but keeping the letters small and not capitalized. Any significant aspect (in this book the aspects which initiate phases of a cycle are used) is represented simply by its pure number on the circle of 360 degrees. Of course, no "aspect" reaches a greater number than 180 because every aspect after conjunction is also repeated backwards after opposition. In this book, the quadrants are represented by large numbers from 1 to 4. They are circled so they stand out from the house numbers. They are also accompanied, at some points, by the distinguishing symbol Z1, Z2, Z3 and Z4. This letter-number symbol means "Zone 1, Zone 2," etc. in a computer code system designed for use with an individuality profile that is written out in English rather than astrological symbols. The profile is a simple way of putting the birth chart before the novice's eyes without using symbols with which he is unfamiliar. It is part of another series of books designed for use with Cosmopsychology.

symbols in   **use**

saturn in the quad- rants

EXPERIENCE A GROWTH IN ESSENTIAL BEING by defining your self-awareness and self-projection, defining your awareness and projection in substance, defining the extension of your awareness and projection into your immediate surroundings (Saturn, by transit, is moving through the first Quadrant of the birth chart. When it enters the "sign" located there, even if it is not yet there by "degree" of Ascendant, this process begins in a definition of the "attitude" that will be defined in the overall process--the attitude represented by the "sign" on the Ascendant or first house cusp.)

THE CONSTRUCTIVE APPROACH is to realize that for a number of years ahead (the number of years it will take Saturn to move through the number of "degrees" of sign contained within the first quadrant, which encompasses the first three "houses") you are going through A PERSONAL GROWTH IN DEPTH. You will come to know yourself as you may never have known yourself before. Until this time, you have held the influence of your family- or society-status (if Saturn has not been through this quadrant yet during your lifetime) and your growth has been proceeding OUTWARD, in response to the conditions of your environment. Now, it must proceed INWARD. If you realize you are building a psychological body of attitudes that will shape the next 30 years of your life, you will also realize that this is the best time of your life for an "education," either a formal one where you come to know yourself in society's intellectual terms, or an "education in life" where you come to know a new self in terms of your surroundings. If this is the second time Saturn has been through this part of your birth chart since you were born, it is time to realize that IT'S IMPORTANT TO DEVELOP NEW RESPONSES TO LIFE, to go through an individual rebirth of awareness of yourself, the reality of yourself and the ability to extend yourself outward into your environment.

THE MATTERS THAT WILL BE STRESSED DURING THIS PERIOD are what you are projecting outward about yourself, the "realism" of that projection, and the flexibility of it in coming to terms with immediate issues in your mind, your close family and your ability to "relate" personally, and intellectually, to anyone or any situation which is part of your surroundings.

THE USUAL MANIFESTATION of this transit is (first time Saturn moves in this quadrant) that the individual is disciplined in his appearance and projection, taught to handle his personal resources (whether material or psychological) and experiences either depth, or frustration, in the personal learning processes in which he is engaged. Another manifestation, and the most common one (when Saturn passes through this quadrant for the second time) is that individuals who have been "riding high" on the influence they have achieved or inherited (and if Saturn was in the first quadrant AT BIRTH this can happen in its first transit in this quadrant) and they suddenly come to realize, sometimes in very shattering ways, that "influence is deserting them." Many people, riding high, and not realizing that a time of personal re-definition is coming, ride TOO high--change jobs with a fickle abandon and suddenly find themselves OUT of a job. Anything one held before he came into this transit of the first quadrant is extremely difficult to attain again in the same material dimension once the transit has begun. Many fall from esteem in others' eyes. Many feel that "the end has begun." It hasn't. And yet, in a way, it has because the END OF AN OLD IDENTITY AND ROUTINE OF BEING ACCEPTED FOR WHAT YOU WERE has come to an end. You must begin to know yourself in depth. If it requires the loss of job, status, or any kind of personal influence to shatter your ego enough that this can be accomplished, then circumstances will provide that requirement. YOUR MUST RELEARN YOURSELF AND YOUR PERSONAL CAPACITIES DURING THIS PERIOD for you are going to become a new person--in one way or another--whether you like it or not.

EXPERIENCE GROWTH BY REDEFINING YOUR AWARENESS AND PROJECTION OF IT (Saturn is transitting the first house). Get to know the real individual inside. (Get to know the potential of Uranus at your birth.) Start bringing it to the outside through the individuality you actually possess (the degree of your Ascendant) in projecting yourself and becoming aware of what you ARE projecting. It's time for you to become something other than "what you were taught." The way you see yourself as "separate from others," the way you think you are personally unique in that respect (you natal Saturn's nature) is going to have to be redefined if you are to go on in life, now, and meet the potential in you that you may NOT have been taught.

THE USUAL MANIFESTATION (of Saturn transitting the first house) is that the individual feels a "loss of self-confidence." Sometimes he feels his "usual vitality" has deserted him. Many people go into deep depressions because "something that was there before is eluding them." They suffer a loss of prestige and sometimes of people and things in their life. They stand alone, now, and the reason is that THEY MUST DEFINE, OR REDEFINE, JUST WHO THEY ARE AND WHAT THEY INTEND TO DO WITH IT IN THE YEARS AHEAD.

EXPERIENCE GROWTH BY DEFINING THE SUBSTANCE OF YOURSELF. How REALLY are you trying to be an individual? What does this mean to you materially and emotionally? The psychological nature of your self-awareness and self-projection must now be focalized. You begin to get to know yourself deeply. You want to put substance into what people think of you because of your self-projection and into what you are coming to know of yourself because of a new kind of self-awareness. (This happens when Saturn transits the second house.)

THE USUAL MANIFESTATION (of Saturn transitting the second house) is a need to work harder to PRODUCE both materially and emotionally. Many people experience a cutback in their finances. They have to "work for what they earn," both in personal earnings and in what people see them as "really," in the world's terms. Many times this means that a person "feels" he "doesn't have as much as he would like" to spend--in putting reality into himself in others' eyes and in financial terms.

EXPERIENCE GROWTH BY DEFINING THE EXTENSION OF YOURSELF INTO YOUR SURROUNDINGS (Saturn transits the third house). This is a time when your mind can grow, not in breadth, but in depth. It's a time when you focalize the activities that ARE your extensions into the environment--you ability to communicate with others, your ability to think, your ability to learn, your ability to get along with people who are part of your "family" or your "community." You are defining your EXTENSION OF YOURSELF in all these things. If you ever are going to learn anything deeply, or communicate with profundity, this is the time it is most likely to happen--because circumstances are conspiring to make you deeper as a person. You are about ready to "focalize your activities" and this period of depth in mind will make it possible.

THE USUAL MANIFESTATION (Saturn transits the third house), for many people, is a sense of "mental depression." If this happens in a child's young life, he may have trouble in school. He will find it difficult to communicate, or learn, unless he does so with patience. Unless he takes everything slowly. In an adult's life, it can mean "difficulties with relatives," frustrations in taking part in the community or in any kind of learning programs in which he's involved. For people who will not come to their "personal center" and grasp themselves in a new way, this will be a period of difficulty in all third house matters--which covers personal communications, personal relatives, personal learning, going to school, trying to learn in a "community college" atmosphere (in contrast to learning in a "university" atmosphere), being involved in the community, the neighborhood, or in a close family. This is because PERSONAL EXTENSION OF YOURSELF MUST NOW BE DEFINED SO YOU CAN FOCUS YOUR ACTIVITIES DOWN TO WHAT'S ESSENTIAL FOR YOU TO GET A GRASP ON WHAT YOU'RE REALLY GOING TO DO FROM HERE ON.

saturn in the quad-rants

EXPERIENCE A GROWTH IN PERSONAL CAPACITY by focalizing your activities, defining your personal expressions, and focalizing your ability to adjust to what lies outside your realm of personal involvement (Saturn, by transit, is moving through the Second Quadrant of the birth chart. When it enters the "sign" located on the cusp of the fourth house, even though it may not yet have come to the "degree" there, the attitude represented by the "sign" on the cusp starts to undergo re-definition.)

THE CONSTRUCTIVE APPROACH is to realize that for a number of years now (the number of years it took Saturn to travel through the number of "degrees" in the first quadrant) you have been undergoing a personal rebirth and now, for a number of years ahead, you are going to be emerging into the world around you in some new psychological form because you are UNDERGOING A GROWTH IN PERSONAL EXPERIENCE. You will probably feel somewhat "relieved" that the growth in essential being has reached this point where it can move outward into new experiences that will give you the capacity to operate as a new kind of human being--one who DOES realize what he's capable of and moves toward expressing that before he goes out to function in the world outside himself (when Saturn will enter the fourth quadrant, by transit). If you realize you have finished building a psychological body of personal attitudes and are now living, or testing, them out, you will gain the required insight into what is happening to you now. IT IS IMPORT-ANT, at this point, TO EXERCISE THE NEW RESPONSES TO LIFE that you gained in personal awareness while Saturn transitted the first quadrant. It is time to emerge from personal growth to personal self-expression.

THE MATTERS THAT WILL BE STRESSED DURING THIS PERIOD are home and family or "personal psychological roots and security," the foundations you are operating on personally in life, children, personal loves or creative activity that allows you to express yourself individually, your ability to take personal risks in a calculated, or well-thought-out way, your health, your work, or your ability -- in reality (for that's what health and work really are)--to adjust to what lies outside yourself. And you do this by making yourself an efficiently functioning indi--vidual so you can spend your awareness of what is not you. If there are any parts of you--physically, emotionally, mentally or spiritually--that are not functioning well, they will probably come to your attention during this time. That is happening so that you will be WELL-EQUIPPED TO MEET OPPORTUNITY in the period when you begin to function among others, and in their terms, more than in your own concerns and in your own ways.

THE USUAL MANIFESTATION OF THIS TRANSIT OF THE SECOND QUADRANT is that the individual suddenly feels he has been relieved of a great burden--the burden of reconstructing himself, because of circumstances around him--when he didn't even realize there SHOULD BE such a burden. Most people feel so free that they begin to circulate again, they move out of themselves, they reach out for "experience" and "pleasure." The concentration now is not on self-growth but on self-expression after having gone through a period of what they felt was "something like the roof falling in--it was the worst period of my life." They only say that because they did not take advantage of the enormous possibility that was there to BECOME A NEW PERSON. They were FORCED to become a new person. That's why many, while Saturn transitted the first quadrant, found their funds cut, their mind depressed, little attention paid to them. All these things were necessary to make them realize it was TIME TO REDEFINE THEMSELVES SO THEY COULD REDEFINE THEIR ABILITY TO EXPRESS THEMSELVES (which is happening now). Because the contrast is so great to what should have happened during the previous growth experience, many people feel "released from a binding cage." Well, that cage was simply a definition of what they could be on a renewed basis. And, yes, they are out with it now--out in the world living it out, whatever it has become. Many people feel (because in the northern hemisphere this Saturn transit of the first quadrant can last as long as 10 years) that "I came near dying" during the first quadrant transit "and suddenly life opened up to me again" during the second quadrant transit. Yes, that is true, too. But it depends on what level you perceive dying, and what level you perceive "opening up," to realize that A DEATH OF FORMER ATTITUDES AND ACTIVITY PATTERN HAS BEEN ACCOMPLISHED.

GROW IN CAPACITY BY FOCALIZING YOUR ACTIVITIES (Saturn is transitting the fourth house). It is time to define the boundaries of your operations, to determine just where you "are standing" in this world, personally. It is time to lay the foundations of a new round of expression of yourself in this world and later of expression of yourself in others' eyes. This is a period when you put depth into your personal sense of security. Does "home" mean a feeling, a place, an attitude, a person, or an idea, to you? This is the time to decide. This is the time to lay "the anchor" you will always be able to come back to in the next 20 to 22 years. We could say that you are laying the foundations of your psychological or spiritual body of future activity. Secure the "place you stand personally"--in material, emotional, mental and spiritual terms. And you can do this best by DECIDING WHAT ACTIVITIES YOU WILL MOVE OUTWARD INTO THE WORLD FROM.

THE USUAL MANIFESTATION (Saturn transitting the fourth house) is for the individual to feel "cramped" in his personal surroundings, to become depressed with his family, to find the "flaws" in the home situation relating to his marriage, to feel that his "base of operations" is not adequate. This is simply because he is not responding to what is required by circumstances. It is saying, "focus yourself; know where and how you stand." Necessity brings one into focus. This is why he may feel "cramped" in his surroundings. They aren't big enough--they don't fit adequately what he "senses" is coming. And that's probably right--particularly if they are the same base, the same foundations, the same lodgings, that were there before Saturn entered its transit of the first quadrant of the birth chart. Many people find their homes being devalued, their property developing problems, their plumbing (in the home) falling apart. Some find the "base of their life so far" (their marriage, their home atmosphere) falling apart on them. THIS IS SO THEY WILL CHANGE IT TO MEET THE NEEDS OF THE NEXT DEVELOPMENT.

DEFINE YOUR SELF-EXPRESSION (Saturn is transitting the fifth house) by putting depth into your personal creations, coming to terms with the problems your children may have, moving cautiously in risk-taking, and, especially, REALIZING PROFOUNDLY THAT YOU ARE AN INDIVIDUAL WHO CAN COME TO CREATIVE TERMS WITH LIFE. If you are not serious about it, love can elude you, BECAUSE you are not serious. The need is to define yourself in all fifth house matters. That is, put depth and meaning, into what you are saying about yourself--through your loves, your children, your gambles and your creative activities. If a "writer" were ever going to "get down to the business of writing and turn out his creations in reality," this is the time for it. If a parent were going to understand, with depth, his children, this is the time for it. If a lover were going to encounter a "profound love," this is the time for it. If a teacher were going to realize deeply what her students need, this is the time for it. If an actor, or performer, were going to "work seriously," this is the time for it. Circumstances are conspiring to bring any of this--or all of it--about in your life, depending on who you are and what you're doing in this field of personal activities because this is where you DO express yourself and the time has come to DO IT IN REAL TERMS.

THE USUAL MANIFESTATION (Saturn transits the fifth house) is to feel "lonely" because "the people you love do not love you." This is nonsense. Do you really love them or are you kidding yourself? Yes, it will be harder to have "fun," because you have got to be serious in expressing yourself. Yes, children can prove a "frustration and a trial" because their ACTUAL NEEDS are becoming real. Yes, you will have to "work to create" because YOU ARE DEFINING YOURSELF, for a long time to come, through WHAT YOU DO CREATE. For most people, this transit produces frustration with a lover, a child, an audience, or a risk. Unless he knows what he's doing, it's not a good time to gamble, either, because life is likely to show him that he needs to "define" even his gambling procedures. The best way for circumstances to illustrate this is to create losses that are impressive --in love, in fun, in ease with children, in audience reaction, and in money if one gambles with it. Life is teaching people to be serious in their expressions because THEY MUST IMPRESS THEMSELVES ON OTHERS IN REAL AND PROFOUND WAYS and not simply frivolously as they may have been taught. This calls for an expression of the real, individual you, in ways that are NOT "the ones that always worked before."

FOCUS YOUR ABILITY TO ADJUST TO WHAT LIES OUTSIDE YOU (Saturn is transitting the sixth house). It's time to realize that you have defined, or redefined, yourself in all personal ways. What excesses have you not taken care of, what parts of you are not operating smoothly and efficiently? It's time to find out because you are getting ready to go out and perform the major function of your life in relation to other people (when Saturn enters the third quadrant). This is the last chance to DEFINE your human capacities before you FUNCTION OUTSIDE YOUR-SELF. Is the work you're doing really a part of what you want to be? Is your health an asset rather than a liability? Do you KNOW HOW TO BECOME AWARE OF OTHERS AS WELL AS YOURSELF? This can be an extremely analytical time when all your excesses and malfunctions are closely examined, because life does not want to send you out a cripple to function in the world beyond your own personal perceptions. DEFINE YOUR SELF-ADJUSTMENTS, FOCUS THEM INTO AN EFFECTIVE METHOD. You will need to know you are "functioning properly" in the tasks that are ahead.

THE USUAL MANIFESTATION (Saturn transitting the sixth house) is a feeling that your "vitality is lowered," that your "work is boring and self-defeating," that you are "under pressure" from the people who employ you, that "your health is deserting you." All of these are imaginary, unless THERE IS SOMETHING WRONG THAT SHOULD BE ADJUSTED NOW. Yes, your "usual vitality" is being lowered because you are economizing it. If there are any defective parts of your body, they can come to your attention now. If your "job," or "work" is not really suited to what lies ahead in your experience, you probably will become "depressed" with it. THIS IS A CRITICAL STATE OF THIS PART OF YOUR EXISTENCE. From here on, you are going to function out in the world of "others" and "society." You are going to build your place in the world, or the "image" you will live on the record. You will NEED to be self-adjusted, and functioning efficiently (or as efficiently as possible) in order to do this because YOU HAVE GONE THROUGH AN EXPERIENCE OF GROWTH IN BEING AND GROWTH IN CAPACITY and now it is going to be put out into the world to see what it can do there IN FUNCTIONING AMONG OTHERS.

(One note must be made at this point. If there are many planets below the horizon, in the birth chart, at your birth, then this growth in being and capacity will involve not only your activities in life, but PARTS OF YOUR PERSONALITY as well. If this is so, the NEED for definition, the pressure that circumstances can throw at you to get you to realize that need, can be double in nature. People who have many planets in these two quadrants of personal experience go through much more PERSONAL PRESSURE in coming to terms with a new kind of individual activity-expression. They "feel" it tremendously inside themselves. They are the ones who are most likely to feel, during Saturn's transit of the bottom half of the chart, that "life is against me" if they cannot realize their constantly changing center. Persons born with many planets ABOVE the horizon will probably not feel this at all in the same way. They will experience SOCIAL PRESSURE while they are trying to grow in their activities in the world. What both will have to do is define parts of their personality while they are defining their activities. In the first case, this definition of personality functions is happening at the same time that PERSONAL activities are being defined. The pressure is ON THE PERSON. In the second case, the definition of personality functions is happening at the same time that SOCIAL activities are being defined. Only HALF the pressure is on the person inside. It is, thus, "easier," in most cases (particularly when individuals have no awareness of their real potential) for persons with many planets in the upper hemisphere of the chart to "get through" the Saturn transits without much loss of social status. Since we seem to value that so highly, it might seem that God has singled them out for rewards. The God INSIDE, however, has no such reward conception. The people who go through double personal pressures COULD BE going through double depth of growth--and becoming extremely strong individuals because of it. That's what's hoped for, but, in most cases, that is not what "appears" to be happening, although it actually does. A person who has double pressure on "himself," inside and outside, becomes doubly strong as the result of it "in himself." Yes, and "deeper" and "more profound" in his awarenesses.

EXPERIENCE A GROWTH IN FUNCTIONING by defining your awareness of others, defining the substance of this and then defining a projection of what this means into the surroundings outside your own personal realm of influence (Saturn, by transit, is moving theough the third Quadrant of the birth chart. When it enters the "sign" located on the seventh house cusp, this process begins in a definition of the attitude and substance of the person represented by this sign in his makeup, even though the activity definition of seventh house matters may not begin until Saturn reaches the "degree" of sign on that house).

THE CONSTRUCTIVE APPROACH is to realize that for a number of years ahead (the number of years it will take Saturn to move, by transit, through the number of degrees contained between the seventh and tenth house cusps) you are going through a growth in YOUR ABILITY TO FUNCTION IN THE WORLD OUTSIDE YOU. The long process of self-growth is over. It is time to build your place in the world, whether this place is based on a marriage, a career, a public life or whatever it will be. While growth, before, has been proceeding inward, it now must proceed OUTWARD. If Saturn was located in the first quadrant at your birth, this movement outward can begin in your very early life, not so much in "career" terms as in being recognized for what you do that affects others. If it were located in the fourth Quadrant at your birth, you can move outward at about the age of 15 years. If you were born with the latter condition, you should become aware that at the age of 30, you will have an INWARD growth process that begins things all over for you. Some very "precocious" children are born with this position and do not emerge again, into the limelight, until they are about 45. Everyone wonders what happened to them. If Saturn were in the early part of the third quadrant at birth, your first real outward movement can begin around the age of 30 and you may be considered a "late bloomer." Wherever it was, we can see WHEN IT IS MOST APPROPRIATE FOR YOU, BY AGE, TO MOVE OUT INTO SOCIETY TO BEGIN YOUR MAJOR WORK THERE. That is appropriate when Saturn crosses the seventh house cusp. The emphasis MUST, in some way, go off personal growth and move toward growth in others' eyes, whether this is one other (the life partner) or many others (the public of your life).

THE MATTERS THAT WILL BE STRESSED DURING THIS PERIOD are what you are doing in light of the fact that you are not alone in the world and should now be aware of it in your ACTIVITIES, the ability to destroy your own personal limitations --and one of them is to THINK you are the only person in the world--through the contacts with others that mark your life, and the ability to grow mentally because you come across ideas that are beyond a self-centered atmosphere. Marriage, public activities, partnership matters and finances, psychological depths of yourself in relation to others, religion, philosophy, travel, education--all are stressed as activities during this transit, all are stressed as coming under a need for DEFINI-TION in order that you leave a record of your functioning outside yourself.

THE USUAL MANIFESTATION OF THIS TRANSIT (the first time Saturn moves in this quadrant--unless it started there and, if it did, we would relate these same things to a child's life, in children's ways, rather than in adult ways) is that the person feels "cramped" in his relations with others, "frustrated with his marriage," in over his head in partnership financial matters, baffled as to why others do not any more see things as he does. Many marriages break up when Saturn transits the seventh house, in particular; then the problems come over the "finances" related to the marriage when it travels through the eighth; and, finally, legal matters involv-ing the ruined relationship come to a final head when Saturn transits the ninth house. This only usually happens because the individuals WILL NOT LEARN THAT FUNCTIONING OUTSIDE THE PERSONAL REALM IS THE MOST IMPORTANT THING NOW. Other people find themselves going through "psychological breakdowns" in some kind of work they've been accustomed to for a long time. Still others find themselves breaking away from old religions, having extreme trouble with "going to college." Again, all these things happen because whatever the "trouble" is with is an old and set pattern that NOW MUST BE DEFINED SO THE INDIVIDUAL REALLY KNOWS WHAT HE'S DOING THAT IS ACTUALLY AFFECTING OTHERS. All actions that are done here, out of personal gratification, rather than out of "awareness of others," are likely to be fraught with trouble and frustration. The

saturn in the quad-rants

wholeness of life is saying "it is now appropriate to REALIZE WHAT you are doing in life that is affecting others and leaving an impression on their world." Have you really considered that? Is what you're doing related at all to your actual potential, to your ability to do something that will benefit not just yourself and your personal gratification but the others you live among, too? If you can answer that question, deeply, affirmatively, this transit should pose you no problems. If you cannot, then the "troubles and frustrations" are to set you on the course of your actual potential. There are a number of things you need to define and focus.

FOCUS YOUR AWARENESS OF OTHERS AND DEFINE ITS MEANING (Saturn is transitting the seventh house). If you don't really know the person you've been living with, it's likely that you will come to know him or her now. If you don't truly understand the public you're dealing with, it will probably make you aware of it now. If you are in business, this is a time to define what you're really doing there and what your goals are that are of benefit to the community in which you're operating. Focus your awareness on the others around you. What are they for in your life and what are you for in theirs? Define this in ways that fit your true potential and you will have taken the first important step outside yourself.

THE USUAL MANIFESTATION (of Saturn transitting the seventh house) is "problems in marriage," frustrations with business, feeling that your "public" does not really understand you. Many marriages break up under this transit because one of the partners suddenly realizes it has been "a marriage of convenience" and this is a great revelation. Sometimes marriages break simply because the partners WILL NOT define the purpose of the relationship. Others fold because one partner begins going through a difficult period and the other feels it is "stretching himself too far" to tolerate the other's misfortune. The strangest thing of all is that after this transit is over, many people who have separated get back together again because they "realized what the other person actually had meant to me." This happened because the person refused to DEFINE the relationship in the first place and, instead, found it FRUSTRATING and a burden. Nevertheless, the results of the transit CAUSED a definition--and all those definitions did not end up in negative terms to what the individual felt was his true function.

FOCUS THE SUBSTANCE OF YOUR AWARENESS OF OTHERS AND DEFINE IT (Saturn is transitting the eighth house). It is time to be "realistic" about what you have learned from your relationships. What has come out of them that has helped you to destroy your own personal limitations? What is it you are really trying to PRODUCE in life through your associations with other individuals and your relations with others in general? It's time to DEFINE THE SUBSTANCE OF YOUR OWN PSYCHOLOGICAL STATE as a result of your contacts with ideas or people outside yourself. This is an excellent time to make your contacts with groups of people, geared to a common goal, real and productive. It's a good time, in mundane matters, to define the areas of your partnership finances, to curb your investments and partnership outlays in ORDER to define them. What are they all for? Where are they heading? We can say this about ANY kind of eighth house matter. The time has come to define what others have done to your life. Relatives may die during this transit. The PURPOSE for this happening is so that you can DEFINE WHAT THEY DID IN YOUR LIFE. Even death has its reasons. And so does the death of your own isolated ego. Whatever happens now is trying to accomplish just that. It's time to realize you live in a world peopled by others as well as yourself and all events are leading to that profound realization. You will not be equipped to hold "influence" (the next quadrant transit) if you don't realize this deeply and meaningfully.

THE USUAL MANIFESTATION (Saturn is transitting the eighth house) is, in case a marriage broke up, frustrations and difficulties for the partner who had become blithely dependent upon the finances involved in it; "problems" with partnership finances, inheritances, taxes, all investments because the person DOES NOT REALIZE how instrumental the resources he holds with others actually are to his own life style. Sometimes relatives, or people close to one, do die. What is happening to the person who stands outside the death, but experiences it, is the

REALIZATION OF WHAT OTHERS MEAN TO HIM. Some people get themselves blithely and deeply into occult, or psychological groups, that seem to be a great "drag" on their lives. THIS happens to show them that you do not PLAY AROUND with the power of groups, but you define its effect on you and FOCUS IT INTO YOUR LIFE in some meaningful manner. The most profoundly difficult thing that happens to most people during this period is that they DO go through a destruction of their own personal limitations, during this transit, as a result of what their relationships "produced" for them. This is often felt as painful but it is painful, again, only to the isolated ego that is not aware of the importance of its contacts with others, the seriousness of them, the depth of them, and the need to focus them into their lives in meaningful, rather than frivolous, ways.

FOCUS YOUR HIGHER IDEAS AND DEFINE THEM (Saturn is transitting the ninth house). It is time to learn deeply those ideas that connect you to others, that make your world of awareness wider and deeper. It is time to take your religion or your beliefs, seriously. If you are going to school (beyond public school) it is time to define yourself in educational terms (a process that seems to give most people a kind of pain because the Twentieth Century educational process often discourages oneself from defining himself). If you're a traveler, it's time to focus your activities to see that they are meaningful. It is time to define, and focus, all the CONNECTIONS YOU HAVE OUTSIDE YOUR OWN PERSONAL WORLD.

THE USUAL MANIFESTATION OF THIS TRANSIT (Saturn transitting the ninth house) is that higher education becomes "frustrating." Some people drop out of college because they CANNOT or WILL NOT define themselves and what they're doing there. What is it all for? Some people become frustrated with their religion. IT CAN'T define themselves, either. Many people go through lawsuits because they have not troubled to define the connections they have been making outside their own personal affairs. Many others go through "problems and troubles" with "foreigners" in their lives. Again, because they didn't define the reasons they were there. Others have "difficulty" with travel because they didn't focus it to any kind of goal. ANYTHING THAT IS DONE FRIVOLOUSLY during this transit makes it "difficult" outside your own personal world. THE REASON IS that you are about to GROW IN INFLUENCE and the wholeness of the system does not want you to be a worthless holder of it. It wants you to define your worth to what lies outside you because you are now ABOUT TO BUILD YOUR PERSONAL RECORD IN THE WORLD upon that worth which will come to be known as "your influence outside yourself." This transit, of the ninth house, just before that begins is the last chance life has to urge you to DEFINE YOUR IDEAS, FOCUS YOUR CONNECTIONS OUTSIDE YOURSELF, MAKE REAL THE PHILOSOPHY YOU CARRY OUT TO OTHER MEN, PUT DEPTH INTO YOUR BELIEFS. Are your ideas worth influence? Are your connections defined enough to make your influence stable? Is your philosophy one that will be of worth to others? Are your beliefs profound enough to carry the weight of influence?

(AT THIS POINT YOU HAVE REACHED THE PEAK OF OPPORTUNITY THE WORLD OUTSIDE YOU HOLDS FOR YOU. From this point on, you will hold the influence you have gained from GROWING THROUGH AWARENESS OF OTHERS OUTSIDE YOUR PERSONAL SELF. You now reach the top as the result of the relationships you have made, what you have produced for yourself and others through them, and the extensions you have made into the community or the world, rather than you "immediate environment" (the ninth house in contradistinction to the third). This could be the community or world of ideas to which you belong because of the awarenesses you have achieved and the "body of psychological depth" you have built through them. It doesn't matter what it is. What has happened is this: you have gone out into the world, been affected by it, had some effect upon it and now the activity will be solidified in some POSITION, some "image" on the record of you, some social "role" you will play to hold influence in the world outside yourself. All Saturn has been asking you, through a growth in definition and focus-- if that's what it was; through a growth in depth of awareness--if that's what it was; through a realization of the profundity of the life around you--if that's what it was; or through a valley of personal frustration, difficulty and FORCED growth...all that

saturn in the quad-rants

Saturn, the system's force of definition, has been asking, is this:

ARE YOU WORTH (in terms of the wholeness to which you belong) THE INFLUENCE THAT NOW CAN BE YOURS?

EXPERIENCE A GROWTH IN INFLUENCE by focusing your role and image among others, by defining your foundations in society (or simply outside yourself), by defining and focusing the expression of others through you, and, finally, by defining and focusing the self-adjustment that you must make in order to begin a new cycle of self-definition, or defining the social adjustments you must make in order to do the same, whether this is in life or out of it (Saturn is transitting the "sign" that is on the tenth house cusp and the process of attitude definition required here begins when Saturn enters the sign while the actual definition of the activities comes in depth when Saturn enters the "degree" of sign on the house cusp).

THE CONSTRUCTIVE APPROACH is to realize that for a number of years now you have been building your place in society, or your image in others' eyes, by a gradual process of transformation in which you went outside of personal self and became aware of all the other selves in which you are involved outside your own personal world. You have been MOVING OUTWARD and now comes the time when you BUILD YOUR FOUNDATIONS OUT THERE IN THAT WORLD. Now comes the time when you "focus the image" you are forming in others' eyes, on the public record, in the spiritual realm of world-activity, because at this point the FUNCTIONING begins to give way to the INFLUENCE that comes as a result of it. If you have LEARNED to function IN "awareness of others as well as yourself" this can be one of the most successful periods of your life--in whatever way you measure success. If you HAVE NOT learned to function IN "awarenesss of others," but still cling stubbornly to the thought that you are all that counts, then what you build out there is going to reflect that. A lot of the world's great dictators came to the top of the hill and then rolled down its other side on this transit. They did that because IT FINALLY WAS FOCALIZED IN OTHERS' EYES JUST WHAT THEY WERE DOING. Their foundations were so obviously ego-centered that people began to see them for what they were. And they, being that ego-centered, did not want to stop. They wanted to move on. It is difficult to EXTEND beyond the point you have reached as this transit begins. It is perfectly functional to CONSOLIDATE what you have built, to define it, to focalize it, to enjoy its influence until Saturn moves back to the first house cusp. But if you try to PUSH BEYOND -- except in abstract ways -- your little structure is likely to start tumbling JUST BECAUSE YOU ARE PUSHING WHAT YOU BUILT. You should be making it concrete.

THE MATTERS THAT WILL BE STRESSED DURING THIS PERIOD are the image you are projecting to others, the status you have achieved, the "name" you are leaving on the records, the friendships and associations you make as a result of having built some foundation in society, the aspirations you have to express others --the common goals of them--through yourself, any kind of public life you have built (if that was in your nature--to work for a government, an instituton, a great conglomeration of people moving toward some common goal), the "end of a cycle of growth," the "things there are still to be settled," sickness if your path has been one that built that for you, "confinement" if you have outraged society or the God within, and "everything that must be adjusted so that you can go on to a new cycle of personal awareness and projection." Yes, even "karma," if that is what you believe in.

THE USUAL MANIFESTATION of this transit (the major time that Saturn moves in this quadrant) is that the individual simply feels "I've gone as far as I can go; it must be over." Others, through trial, struggle and frustration, finally reach the goal they set out toward at some previous time--five to ten years before, and they feel they have "finally made it." Some "come to the end of the rope" with what they have been doing--it appears disillusioning, frustrating and barren of meaning, because IT WASN'T WHAT THEY REALLY THOUGHT IT WOULD BE. That's be-cause they never thought of defining it, they didn't focus on what they were actually building and, to be perfectly frank, they didn't learn a damned thing as a result of the interaction of others in their life--whereas it could have made them into entirely different people, perfectly capable of holding influence meaningfully among others when they REACHED A GOAL THAT HAD MEANING TO OTHERS AS WELL AS THEMSELVES. Actually, the disillusionment manifestation is somewhat uncommon. Most people DO reach the top of the heap during this transit, even if after the presentation of the trophy it begins to gather dust BECAUSE A GROWING REALIZATION SETS IN THAT IT MIGHT NOT HAVE BEEN WORTH ALL THE STRUGGLE. And why was that? Because the goal had nothing to do with their actual potential. It was simply a "standard" set by society or by ideas outside one's own potential. Many people, I must say, also, reach the peak of their efforts--and DO feel satisfied in themselves--even if the world does not like it...partly because the world wasn't ready for them. But USUALLY the world is. And if this is a hollow victory, it is because the goal was hollow inside the person in relation to what he came into the world equipped potentially to do. If you experienced this, at one point in your life--the hollowness of the victory--what could you have done to make it different?

FOCALIZE YOUR IMAGE AMONG OTHERS, DEFINE ITS WORTH (Saturn is transitting the tenth house). It's time to focus what you're doing in whatever position you're holding professionally, in a career, or simply in the eyes of the community or of people in general. You need, now, to define, and make profound, your relation to everything that's outside your personal life. This is usually the time when a career or profession comes to a peak of success or achievement. It's a time when the individual engaged in that success is asked, by everything around him, to be responsible in what he's doing. Whatever has been building, in one's outer life, since Saturn began its transit on from the seventh house now comes to a head.

THE USUAL MANIFESTATION (of Saturn transitting the tenth house) is for the individual to feel "pressured" in his career, to feel that he has many "burdens and responsibilities" that he didn't realize before. This is only a negative reaction to what's happening. These burdens and responsibilities become heavy because he needs to DEFINE what he's doing, ECONOMIZE on his procedures and MAKE REAL the meaning of the tasks in which he is engaged. Many people, in their jobs, feel "pressure" from their superiors. Others feel that they, of all the people around them, are being asked to carry responsibilities that they really don't want. Some individuals simply feel, suddenly, that what they are doing is "empty of meaning" because they have no definition, in themselves, of what it's for, that's beneficial, in their own life goals. There is always a feeling of pressure when one is FORCED TO DEFINE what he's doing. If, however, he CHOOSES to do this, there then is often a feeling of depth and worth in what he's doing.

DEFINE YOUR EXPRESSION THROUGH OTHERS AND FOCUS YOUR ASSOCIATIONS (Saturn is transitting the eleventh house). It is time now to realize how you are expressing your role in society through others and how, in reverse, their common needs are being expressed through you. It is time for you to define this so you can understand it and focus it so that you know what you are doing with it. What has been the RESULT of your career, your profession, the foundations you have built in society? What have they done for you and, through you, to others? You will probably see this in very realistic terms, one way or another, during this transit. If you have achieved what your potential made you capable of doing in the community, in your own field of endeavor, in the eyes of others, this will undoubtedly be a time of reward for you. You will feel you have neared the end of a long cycle of work or achievement and you will begin to realize, in very profound terms, what it has all meant--through the associations you now have that are defining forces in your life, through the profound understanding of what your "public role" has promulgated, through the realization that you, as well as anyone, have HAD actual hopes and aspirations to express something of everyone's common need through what you were doing. During this transit, the SUBSTANTIAL REALIZATION of what "influence" you have actually built comes home very strongly to you--either negatively or positively, as you see it, according to what you have actually built in your community, your profession, your world, or whatever group of people or ideas you have partici- pated in beyond your own personal growth and expression.

THE USUAL MANIFESTATION OF THIS TRANSIT (Saturn transitting the eleventh
house)--and it must be apparent by now that when I have been saying "usual manifestation" I have been implicitly suggesting the fact that the person probably has not understood himself and is bumbling through rather than acting in a conscious cycle of
activity--is that one feels "frustrated" by his friends, his associations, the results
of his career or profession and feels the world around him has placed great "weights"
upon his being. If his foundations in society WERE hollow, then this is the payoff
period. The realization of that comes out in rather stark terms--in what you might
call a "shattering" of his hopes and aspirations; the ones he held inside that he never
built toward in any tangible fashion. This can be an extremely bitter period of the
life for an individual who has moved on Saturn's energy since it left the seventh house
cusp and followed society's ideas of what he should do or be, especially if those
ideas had nothing at all to do with his own potential. Now, the REAL EXPRESSION
of the common good he has done through his work becomes all too obvious. If it has
been nothing, it will probably show. If it has been something, it will probably show
in deep and real ways. The people who "groan" through this transit are the ones
who will UNDOUBTEDLY HAVE TO DEFINE THEMSELVES ENTIRELY ANEW--
inside themselves while Saturn transits the twelfth house; and into their surroundings
in new awarenesses and new projections when Saturn begins once more its cycle
of the whole field of attitudes to the outer world when it moves over the Ascendant.

DEFINE THE SELF-ADJUSTMENTS YOU MUST MAKE IN ORDER TO BEGIN A
NEW CYCLE OF AWARENESS AND PROJECTION (Saturn is transitting the twelfth
house). It is time to go inside yourself, to withdraw (at least in your mind) from
the previous cycle of activity and decide where you now want to go. You stand at
this moment between two great cycles. If this is an early part of your life, you
stand at the end of being, instinctively, what you were born--and however that was
shaped or mis-shaped by the influences around you in your growing up. If this is
the middle part of your life, the former could be true, or another thing could be
true: You have achieved in the world outside yourself and it is time now for you to
consider how you can grow even beyond that, how you can begin taking yourself out
of social awareness and into the kind of awareness that goes beyond that--the kind
of awareness that lets you make contact with greater worlds of perception. If
this is the latter part of your life, you have probably achieved as much as is possible for an individual and it's REALLY time to get out of that and into contacts with
whatever will sustain you through the last part of your life. Whatever the case is,
ANYONE, at this point, stands at the critical juncture of the cycle where he must
begin to adjust himself out of outer activity and back into inner growth. It can feel
like a time of withdrawal or confinement (inside yourself) while you do this. The
old astrologers called this the "house of karma." Well, yes, and what happens when
Saturn transits it is that the individual is brought to face "the causes he has set in
motion in his own life." Sometimes, these things come up mysteriously from what
has been done in other lives. In either case, it is time to make the adjustments
necessary to realize deeply inside yourself just where you have been and what you have
achieved, because it's time to prepare for a rebirth in awareness of the world around
you and your eventual relation to it.

THE USUAL MANIFESTATION OF THIS TRANSIT (Saturn moving in the twelfth) is
that the individual feels "fate" has come on him with a heavy hand. He feels "confined"
and doesn't know why. The only reason is that if he has not yet learned how to respond
to the defining energies that move toward the earth from the Solar System's outer-
most planet, then he will probably be FORCED to come face to face with them in
very ego-shattering ways. Saturn is NOT THE "TASKMASTER" as many have called
it; it is the "timekeeper" of the wholeness's process of growth through human beings.
And when it sends energy to this field of his individual makeup it is simply saying
to him, IT IS TIME TO ADJUST YOURSELF TO THE FACT THAT A NEW CYCLE
OF INDIVIDUAL ACTIVITY IS ABOUT TO BEGIN. Many individuals are not only
ignorant, but stubborn (and I know because I have been one of them), and they
stupidly "harvest their own worst products" during this period. They accept the
"confinement" but they decide to "get even" for it. And this is the worst attitude one
could possibly take at this time, because one is still in an "influence" period and
that influence is also soon going to leave him.

THE TWELFTH HOUSE TRANSIT OF SATURN IS ONE WORTH REMARKING ON MORE because it is one of the critical points in an individual's ability to realize-- through force or through his own perception--that there is a timing to the cycles that go on in the wholeness of the system and this timing is applying to his own life. When Saturn moves through that part of the sky that represents the twelfth field of activities in his life, it shows BY SIGN the DEFINITION OF ATTITUDE that will make it possible for him to readjust himself to what lies outside him. It also shows, by its aspect and phase, to its birth position in his chart, just what the "purpose" of this is, now, in a long cycle of individual structuring that has been going on in him. He stands, at this point, at the threshold of two worlds of activity--the one he is leaving behind, and on the record; and the one he's about to enter and which will eventually end up., also, on the record. Because of this, it would be beneficial to himself if he could see, overall, what happens in the personal growth cycle of definition that Saturn is continually moving on and resetting in motion in his life.

LET'S LOOK AT IT AGAIN, IN RETROSPECT:

During its transit of the First Quadrant, Saturn calls into being the need for a GROWTH IN ESSENTIAL BEING. This is for one of two reasons, if he has lived during the time that it transitted the part of the sky represented, in his birth sky, in the fourth quadrant of his birth chart. The first, and most common reason, is that a growth in essential being IS ABSOLUTELY NECESSARY if this individual is ever going to COME NEAR the potential his birth chart held. That suggests that he probably had a hollow, meaningless, growth in influence while it transitted his fourth quadrant and that he now will be forced to COME TO TERMS WITH HIS REAL SELF IN NEW WAYS. This is what causes the First Quadrant, for most people, to become "the obscurity cycle" that Grant Lewi called it. But it certainly doesn't have to be. If one "grew in influence" with depth and meaning, in the fourth quadrant Saturn transit, it will probably be a kind of relief to get out of activities outside one- self and come to know himself in new, potentially more meaningful, dimensions. The transit of the first quadrant then is a welcome thing--giving one time to relearn his individual potential and redevelop it, before setting out on a new cycle of activity in the world outside himself (when Saturn finally crosses the seventh house cusp).

During its transit of the Second Quadrant, Saturn is giving the individual the ability to "express himself" (and this IS a growing in human capacity) so that he can go out into the world and function there. Many people get so deeply into "expressing themselves" rather meaninglessly that they are entirely unprepared for the fact that it is "time to go out and function in the world around you" (when Saturn enters the third quadrant) and this is why so many marriages fall apart when that transit begins. The "growth in capacity" has somehow been avoided for a "determination to express myself," and, probably, we could add, "the worst side of myself." It is right here, in the transit of the second quadrant that one lays a lot of the eggs that are going to hatch when Saturn crosses the seventh house cusp. It is very important to grow in self-expression but THE EVENTUAL GOAL of this growth is to propel one out into the world around him to FUNCTION THERE. It is not to stay here, in self-satisfaction, forever and ever. And yet, that's just how many take it, and just how many are "crushed" under Saturn's "heavy revelations" when it moves into the third quadrant.

During the transit of the Third Quadrant, Saturn is giving the individual the oppor- tunity TO REALIZE HIMSELF BY PUTTING AWARENESS OF OTHERS FIRST. That means that you start conceiving of yourself in terms of the world that exists around you. You ARE an individual but that individuality was developed so you COULD RELATE IT TO THE SITUATION IN WHICH IT IS EXISTING. I am emphasiz- ing this because often, when Saturn transits the seventh house, in particular, the one great realization that is missing for most people is this: If your "marriage" (or your relations with anyone in any way) will help you to build your foundations in soci- ety in ways that ALLOW YOU to relate to others IN AWARENESS OF OTHERS, it is a workable thing and probably will go on. If it is NOT this kind of "marriage" (or relationship), it NEEDS TO BE REDEFINED. BECAUSE WHAT YOU DO NOW WILL AFFECT NOT ONLY YOU BUT ALL OTHERS TO WHOM YOU RELATE.

saturn in the quad- rants

THE TRANSIT OF THE THIRD QUADRANT, and the transit of the sixth house just before it, OFTEN MAKES THE DIFFERENCE IN WHAT WILL HAPPEN in the transit of the twelfth house fifteen years later in the life. If one DOES "adjust himself to what lies outside himself" during the sixth house transit he probably begins, with little trouble, "defining his awareness of others in real terms" when the seventh house transit begins--and this DEFINITION is extremely important to what will happen in the twelfth house, because it is the BEGINNING of a process that WILL END THERE. In other words, if one comes to a realization of how his true potential was made to operate AMONG OTHERS--or realizes "what he has to offer to the world outside himself"--he probably embarks on a course that will be meaningful and fulfilling when it comes to an end and moves on to a new cycle. If he DOES NOT GET THIS REALIZATION he is probably LAYING THE FOUNDATION FOR A STRUCTURE THAT WILL BE SHATTERED at the end of the process. In other words, it is here at the beginning of the transit of the seventh, that YOU MUST HAVE IN MIND WHAT IT IS YOU ARE GOING TO BUILD--and that comes from "realizing, in awareness of others, how what you build will be valuable to them as well as to yourself." This seventh house is often equated with the seventh sign of the Zodiac. And the true meaning of Libra is NOT "harmony and balance" (that's only a POTENTIAL), but "the ability to measure yourself in terms of others or of society or of the great wholeness that lies outside, but can come inside, your own individual awareness." Libra measures its WORTH in terms of society, another individual, or the wholeness to which it belongs. Whether that RESULTS in "harmony" or "balance" is a question that is answered later--often, in the life of the individual, if we equate this house with that sign, when the TIME TO ADJUST TO THE CAUSES YOU HAVE SET IN MOTION comes; when the twelfth house transit begins.

Whatever is set in motion during this transit--you see, it is the individual "grown in being and capacity" who now sets it in motion THROUGH HIMSELF--comes to fruition during the tenth house transit and reaches the point of adjustment and dissolution so the whole process can begin over again. The First and Second Quadrant transits are to DEFINE the individual. The Third and Fourth Quadrant transits are to DEFINE WHAT THE INDIVIDUAL DOES OUTSIDE HIMSELF.

If people could understand they are always operating in one of those defining processes, their lives would probably take on much more meaning.

One more thing that must be realized is that in the total complexity of individual development, it is not merely the houses and quadrants that are involved in the defining process, but the individual parts of the personality (the planets) as well. That is the next step here, but before we proceed to it, we might try to make it clear for ourselves that the house and quadrant transits DEFINE ACTIVITIES and that the planet transits DEFINE PARTS OF THE PERSONALITY. An individual, in him- self, is often engaged most deeply in the functioning of his personality. Society, however, most often judges him on his activities, no matter what is happening inside him. So the house and quadrant transits ARE OFTEN WHAT SHOW ON THE WORLD'S RECORD AND ON OTHERS' PERCEPTION OF THE INDIVIDUAL but the planet transits are OFTEN WHAT THE INDIVIDUAL FEELS MOST PROFOUNDLY IN HIMSELF.

Many individuals will be able to say, with striking recognition, that what is said about Saturn's transits of the planets certainly applied to him, BECAUSE HE FELT IT. He may not realize it, but if he could "look back on the record of what he left as impressions in the world's eyes," there might not be any evidence of this at all outside him. But the evidence of the house and quadrant transits would probably stand out starkly on that record. Because that evidence would show on society's books, on society's record, on society's awareness of the individual. The pains and agonies that come from Saturn's misunderstood defining power on the personality are most exquisitely felt by the individual himself. And he will undoubtedly recognize them. If he really values what he's leaving on the record, though, he had probably BETTER become aware of what the transits of the quadrants and houses are leaving behind him even if he doesn't recognize it so well.

When we come to the consideration of Saturn's transits over the birth planets we are beginning to watch PARTS OF THE PERSONALITY and the activities (houses) and attitudes (signs) they govern (that those natal planets "rule") undergoing development because of the stream of energy being released into the atmosphere by Saturn's transit.

The process that begins when any moving energy-factor focuses on a part of the personality, comes to fruition later when the moving energy-factor crosses through the field of activity that personality factor governs. We can discover what purpose is being carried out, at that time, and even the emphasis of activity it provokes, if we consider the PURPOSE OF THE ENERGY BEING RELEASED and within that purpose THE ACCENT OF THE ENERGY (if there is one).

Let's break that statement down by setting up some technical and astrological definitions of the words and phrasing I have just used.

DEFINITIONS:

A MOVING ENERGY-FACTOR is a "transitting planet."

A FOCUS is a "conjunction," or beginning of a cycle of position.

A PART OF THE PERSONALITY is the "natal planet."

A FIELD OF ACTIVITY is a "house" in the birth chart.

The field the personality factor GOVERNS is the "house" that has on its "cusp" the "sign" the "natal planet RULES."

The PURPOSE of the activity is the meaning of the "phase of cycle" the transitting planet is located in (in relation to the position of the natal planet under consideration) in the part of the cycle of position it is making when it crosses through the "house" that natal planet "rules."

The ACCENT of activity within that purpose is the "aspect" the transitting planet is making WITHIN THE PHASE OF ENERGY-FLOW in the cycle of position when it is passing through the house bearing on its cusp the sign the natal planet "rules."

Now, let's put the same statement together again, with the technical meaning of the words used set in parentheses, and extend what was said.

When we consider the parts of the personality (natal planet) that are undergoing development because of circumstances (because of the transit of a planet in the sky) we need to understand that what is happening now, in this part of the personality, will later manifest in activity (house) and attitude (sign) in the part of individual awareness (field of activity) governed by that part of the personality (ruled by the planet transitted).

When an energy-center in the sky (transitting planet) focuses on (conjoins) one of the personality parts, the moving energy-field is throwing out the possibility that this personality part can now operate in ITS (transitting planet's) terms BECAUSE of the kind of energy it releases to it (the kind of energy the transitting planet releases). The focus of energy (conjunction) by the moving force on the personality part (natal planet) begins a cycle of energy-flow between the two that is not finished until the next focus (next conjunction of the two).

What starts at this point may later be "concretized," made real, or "defined," in the field of activities (the house) the personality part (natal planet) governs (rules). And this happens when the moving energy-center (transitting planet) later contacts the field the personality part governs (transits the house whose cusp bears the sign this natal planet "rules").

When it does this, it releases a purposeful energy flow (operates in a phase of the continuing cycle of position that has been in effect since its conjunction of the natal planet) to that personality part. This energy may be accented in a certain way (there may be an "aspect" made within the "phase") when the moving energy-center passes through the field. This purpose, and accentuation of it, is important because it shows the STATE of the energy being released to define the activities in that field as a result of the PROCESS OF INTERFLOW (the phase of cycle after the conjunction) between the two. It also shows WHERE the process is, in relation to an overall 30-year period of defining the personality part.

There are five important considerations we must make every time we look at a transitting planet making a conjunction, or aspect, with a natal planet, if we are to really understand what can potentially happen in the person as a result of this outside energy merging with his own inner personality energies.

FIRST, we see an INNER ACTIVITY, in the case of the Saturn transit to a natal planet, that is undergoing definition.

SECOND, we realize that this is only the INSTINCTIVE BEGINNING of a 30-year cycle of realization involving that personality part AND the field of activity it governs.

THIRD, we realize that what was started IN THE PERSONALITY, at the conjunction, is not necessarily completed when the transit passes, but CAN COME TO MANIFESTATION LATER (when Saturn transits there) in the activities (house) and attitudes (sign) that natal planet governs in the chart. And this later manifestation comes when Saturn passes through the sign and house that planet governs.

FOURTH, at that later time (though we should try to see it now, when the process begins, to see what it will go through before that later time is arrived at), there will be a PURPOSE (a phase of cycle) active in the manifestation of activities (house transit) that began in the personality part (when the natal planet was transit-ted) when it was focused upon (when Saturn conjoined it).

FIFTH, we can realize that there is, possibly, an ACCENTUATION of purpose (aspect within the phase) that allows the manifestation of activity and attitude to be easy (soft aspect) or challenging (hard aspect).

What I am trying to get you to understand, in the following interpretations, is this: Yes, there is a personality definition going on right here and now, in this activity field (in this house), when Saturn transits the planet IN THAT HOUSE. BUT (and this is most important and seldom seen) THERE IS ALSO BEGINNING A 30-year process of development that can manifest in attitudes and activities in the house the natal planet RULES when SATURN LATER crosses through that house and sign. And we must see this as part of a cycle that began at the conjunction of the natal planet because THE DEFINITION THAT STARTED INSTINCTIVELY THEN (in the house where that natal planet was located) WANTS TO MANIFEST IN ACTIVITY AND ATTITUDE IN THE FIELD THAT PERSONALITY PART GOVERNS (in the house that bears the sign on its cusp that that natal planet rules). And in this manifestation, later, there is a PURPOSE going on and, often, within that purpose, an accentuation of energy flow.

In other words, EVERYTHING we have already talked about in Saturn's transits of the signs, the quadrants and the houses IS RELATED strongly to Saturn's transit of the natal planets. NONE OF THESE THINGS IS UN-RELATED.

If you can understand an attitude being defined (a sign being transitted) you can see WHERE THAT BEGAN in this person by noting when Saturn last conjoined the planet in the chart that rules that sign. If you can understand a field of activities undergoing definition you can see WHERE THAT BEGAN in this person by noting when Saturn last conjoined the planet in the chart that rules the sign on the "cusp" of that house.

If you can understand an awareness being developed (a whole quadrant being activated by the transit) you can see WHERE THE NEED FOR IT BEGAN by noting the planet in the chart that rules the sign on the cusp of that quadrant and going back to the time when Saturn conjoined the planet that rules the sign on that cusp.

Further, and even more important, you can SEE THE PURPOSE AND THE ACCENTUATION OF PURPOSE INVOLVED (the phase and aspect in effect) when any of the above things begins by noting WHERE IN THE CYCLE OF ENERGY FLOW, AND IN WHAT ASPECT, Saturn is now related to the natal planet.

In the following interpretations, we will do all that.

We will first consider the meaning of the conjunction of Saturn with a natal planet. But we will also consider the meaning of the CYCLE OF DEVELOPMENT that began then by noting every important phase and aspect within that cycle and noting when (by subsequent year) the purposes and accentuations of those phases of cycle and aspects within them will occur.

Let me illustrate what I am saying by giving you a personal example that is having a direct effect upon what you are reading.

Back in the early 1960's, Saturn transitted my natal Mercury which is located in the first house of the birth chart. Instinctively, I began a deep process of mental reorientation but all that happened then was not over when the transit was over. In fact, much of what happened then, is only emerging into manifestation and definition, now, when transitting Saturn is moving through the sign and house in the birth chart that my natal Mercury "rules."

Back in the 1960's, I was emerging from college and into politics and the journalistic world. One of the things that most depressed me at that time was that I really could not offer people any good advice for the questions they were posing me. What is life about? What makes sense of it? Where am I going and what will be the result of it? Yet, I got deeply involved in a search for answers to these questions because I, too, felt the need for answers or directions.

What I didn't realize then (because I was a real novice and was making no sense at all of astrology, merely plunging into it and being confused by it) was that I was going through a "growth in essential being" (Saturn was transitting the first quadrant of my birth chart). I was also undergoing a period of "defining my self-awareness and self-projection" (Saturn was in the first house). Inside, I was going through a process of "deepening my thoughts, defining my ability to assimilate the results of social contacts and interactions, and defining my own personal systems for self-adjustment" (Saturn transitting Mercury). But I was also manifesting the worst side of it, too, because I found myself plunging into constant and profound depressions BECAUSE NO ONE COULD EXPLAIN TO ME WHAT WAS HAPPENING TO ME. I have since learned, however.

I was beginning, instinctively, a process of mental definition that would come to fruition in manifestation of new activities and attitudes, particularly in personal self-expression, in 1972 and 1973, when Saturn passed through my fifth house and through the sign Gemini, both of which, in my chart, are ruled by natal Mercury.

When I realize that, I can also see the PURPOSE of what is going on at the current time in 1973. The PURPOSE (the meaning of the phase of the cycle of position in which transitting Saturn is now located in respect to my natal Mercury) is to "perfect my techniques of operation so I can get outside my self-involvement and attempt to do something that is of social worth" (Saturn makes the Gibbous phase by transit to my natal Mercury) and the ACCENTUATION now of that process is "an irritating tendency to veer off course from the goal, or realization, ahead" (Saturn is making a 150-degree aspect to natal Mercury within the Gibbous phase).

your growth in cyclic pattern

Because I am so involved in interpretting other people's birth charts, I hardly ever look at my own. But while I was writing this book on transitting Saturn, I began to realize how profoundly what I was saying to others applies to myself. Everything I am writing today, developed out of the problems and involvements into which I instinctively plunged in my forced mental development back in the early 1960's. Only now is it reaching manifestation in this form. And the problems I am experiencing while writing this are also very clear. I have to learn to "curb my restlessness" (Saturn in Gemini) particularly in "defining" my self-expression" (Saturn in the fifth house) and the PURPOSE OF THIS is "to perfect my techniques of operation so I can get outside self-involvement and make myself of social worth" (Saturn in the Gibbous phase to natal Mercury) and THERE IS the "irritating tendency to veer off course from the goal, or realization, ahead" (Saturn in 150-degree aspect to Mercury within the Gibbous phase to it).

That's what's happening now, as this is being written. If I want to go back, I can look at the preceding process and see how it all applies. And everything started back there when Saturn transitted natal Mercury.

And, if I may say so, that makes a lot more sense to me than the usual interpretation of "being thankful when Saturn gets off your Mercury because then you won't have such a tendency to be depressed." Well, there's a reason for everything. If we're depressed, it's because we're not learning to be profound mentally. Sometimes, it's because we don't know where everything that's happening now, through circumstance and from outer pressures, is leading.

I now know where it's leading in my case and I think that if you follow the course of interpretation ahead you will also be able to find where it's leading in your case. We have nothing, I repeat nothing, to fear from the transits. But our own ignorance is, indeed, a factor that should frighten anyone.

If you go through these interpretations and decide that they are taking a lot of time to understand, I can say only this to you:

How cheap, and how shallow, is your life, or any other man's? Can it really be reduced to the quick, two-second phrase that makes immediate understanding?

I personally doubt it, after having lived this far through a Saturn transit cycle of natal Mercury, and I think that if you consider it you will come to the conclusion that you are a complex being and anything that's going to speak to you truthfully and as fully as it can will at least appear complex, too.

The first thing is to understand the whole cycle of development. It goes through eight phases and many accentuations because of the aspects in effect during those phases. One half of this 30-year development, the first 15 years after the Saturn conjunction of the natal planet, is instinctive and active. You don't think much about it, until Saturn gets near the opposition of the planet. You plunge into what circumstances throw at you. When you reach the opposition a period of 15 years of development in consciousness begins. If it doesn't, if you don't think before you act after that, you are likely to be in trouble and floundering until the next conjunction. If you think I have laid heavy stress upon the cycle and the phases and aspects within them, you are correct. I would hope to give you at least the rudimentary keys that will ALLOW YOU TO MAKE USE OF THE CYCLE rather than merely flounder through it. As I say, it is difficult to consciously understand the first 15 years. But it is imperative to have attained some kind of realization, and make conscious choices about what you'll do, in the second 15 years.

Even if you can't make conscious choices very well in the first 15 years (and I could have, if I had chosen to put my true potential to work because natal Saturn and natal Mercury were in the Last Quarter phase and they could have made that possible if I had not been ignorantly overwhelmed by the stream of energy coming from outside; I HAD TO at least learn to handle it, but I didn't have to succumb entirely to it--and I hope you will remember that about your natal potentials, too, when you consider these transitting developments because of the energy released to you by the transit cycle in effect), you can come to understand what is happening to you and not feel that fate is overwhelming you with forces that are engulfing you and not even revealing what they're for or where they're pushing you.

The cycle of phases of energy-flow, and the aspects forming within them, runs like this:

0	conjunction	(opens NEW PHASE) (beginning of whole cycle)	"the spontaneous beginning"	**NW** **0-45**
30	semi-sextile	(part of new phase) (2-3 years later)	"merging of two polarities of thought or action"	
45	semi-square	(opens CRESCENT phase) (3 to 4 years later)	"mobilization forward from the past line of activity"	
60	sextile	(part of Crescent) (4 to 5 years later)	"production in the forward movement"	**CR** **45-90**
72	quintile	(part of Crescent) (5 to 6 years later)	"personal creativity in the production"	
90	square	(opens FIRST QUARTER phase) (7 to 8 years after conjunction)	"crisis or challenge, from or to the surroundings"	**FQ** **90-135**
120	trine	(part of FIRST QTR.) (9 to 10 years later)	"creation, or easy flow, after the crisis or challenge"	
135	sesquiquadrate	(opens GIBBOUS phase) (10 to 11 years later)	"challenge to adopt techniques that work in the situation"	**GI** **135-180**
144	biquintile	(part of Gibbous) (11 to 12 years later)	"adoption of personally creative techniques"	
150	quincunx	(part of Gibbous) (12 to 13 years later)	"tendency to become absorbed in technique, veer off course"	
180	opposition	(opens FULL phase) (14 to 15 years after conjunction)	"beginning of conscious action-- adding content, meaning or purpose to activity--or a falling apart of activity"	**FU** **180-135**
150	quincunx	(part of Full) (2-3 years after opposition)	"movement away from realization itself and into conscious activity"	
144	biquintile	(part of Full) (3-4 years after opposition)	"conscious adoption of creative techniques to activity"	
135	sesquiquadrate	(opens DISSEMINATING PHASE) (4-5 years after opposition)	"conscious movement outward into surroundings with message or activity"	**DI** **135-90**
120	trine	(part of DISSEMINATING phase) (5-6 years after opposition)	"easy flow of ideas into the surroundings; creativity in action'	
90	square	(opens LAST QTR. phase) (7-8 years after opposition)	"challenge from inside to re-orient ideas or activity"	**LQ** **90-45**
72	quintile	(part of LAST QTR.) (8-9 years after opposition)	"personal creativity inside"	
60	sextile	(part of LAST QTR.) (9-10 years after opposition)	"inner production of new ideas"	
45	semi-square	(opens BALSAMIC phase) (11 to 12 years after opposition)	"challenge to consciously recreate oneself in mind and activity"	**BA** **45-0**
30	semi-sextile	(part of BALSAMIC) (12 to 13 years after opposition)	"merging of old vehicle with new idea or activity"	

saturn in its main cycle

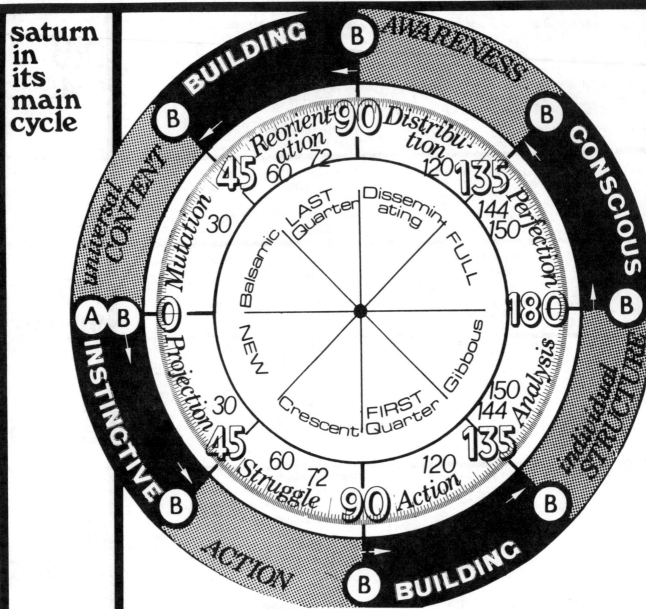

If we start looking at the cycle of Saturn's transits in this way, it will become much more meaningful to us than watching aspects form "separately" and fearing what "they will produce." They will produce nothing that we do not wish if we are in tune with the cycle. If we are not, our own ignorance will produce a lot of difficult things.

The most effective of Saturn's cycles is the cycle of position to its own place because it affects everyone on the same schedule. In fact, it sets up a number of the known rhthyms of development that people follow on a regular society-encouraged basis.

The key ages in a child's development are here in the first part of his life. The key ages of a creative individual's development are here in the second part of his life. And the key ages of a spiritual awareness are here in the third part of the life. Actually, they might not be in the life but they are here in the Saturn cycle. Saturn does not say what we will do with its energy, but it sets the years when the energy will be accented.

Let's just look at a child's life in this light.

Saturn, in the birth chart, is the STRUCTURE of identity. It is the psychological FORM one takes in others' eyes. In the first part of the life this is heavily shaped by society, family and surroundings.

At about 2 to 3 years of age (Saturn's semi-sextile aspect to its birth position), a child learns, often with tremendous effort required, his "name" and his place in the family. At about 3 to 4 years of age, he begins to move out into the community, small as it may seem to him then, with the name. The semi-square aspect is in effect, he is struggling away from the previous life into this one, and he challenges the surroundings with his new name. Many children, at this time, begin to give up the memories they have so strongly and unconsciously about the world before this one. This is the CRESCENT phase of identity development and it is time to give up the "ghosts of the past" that may still cling on unconsciously.

At about 4 to 5 years old, this effort of living out the new name, can be productive with a little effort--children are often introduced to schooling and learning at this time. At 5 to 6 years, when they begin the formal schooling, their personal creative techniques are called upon to reinforce their family-, society-based identity.

At 7 to 8 years of age, there is the challenge of the surroundings through the 90-degree aspect. The child is then expected to move out combatively into his surroundings--either physically or intellectually--and come to terms with it. This is often the "crisis" of the early school years.

At 9 to 10 years of age, the trine aspect sets in and the child can manage rather easily and creatively with his name, his identity, his ability to demonstrate how he is separate from others as an individual.

At 10 to 11 years of age comes the sesquiquadrate aspect where the environment "challenges" him to perfect himself in this identity, to adopt personal techniques that make him personally effective. It is also often a period of "analysis" when the child tries to assert his worth to the family or the community. His personally creative techniques are probably most noticeable at 11 to 12 years of age when the biquintile is operating. And his ability to "veer off course" from coming realizations about how his "identity" is to be consciously used, occurs at about 12 to 13 years of age when the quincunx is effective.

At about 15 years of age, the opposition of Saturn to its birth position occurs. This is the time when a child is expected to become "conscious" of his identity and use his name, and all its resources, consciously and for some purpose. It begins to dawn on him that a 15-year period of instinctive development is over and his mind is developing strongly.

At 16 to 17 years of age, the quincunx again operates and the youngster has an ability to move away from this realization and prepare to do something with it. At 17 to 18 years of age the biquintile is operating and he is expected to use his own personal techniques creatively. And of course, he must. This is the end of the high school years in the United States and secondary education in many societies.

At 18 to 19 years of age, the sesquiquadrate operates and the growing youngster "moves out to challenge his surroundings with this identity that has been perfected and given some idea or activity in which it believes and wants to live out." This is when most youngsters do move out into the world one way or another--to more schooling, to the first realizations of "being on their own with their individual name" or to the working world.

At 20 to 21 years of age, when most youngsters are ready to graduate from college and become "official citizens" the trine aspect operates and it is EASY NOW, or so it seems, to BE AN INDIVIDUAL WITH YOUR OWN NAME. This is when most young people feel freest, when they think they are ready to choose their life course, when society makes it "easier " for them to exist as an individual in his own right. I don't suppose it is entirely ironic that, until recently, the voting age was geared to the second Saturn trine of the first Saturn cycle of position.

At 23 to 24 years of age, the second square of the Saturn cycle begins to operate and there is a "challenge from inside" to abandon the past and begin to real-

saturn in its main cycle

26

nw 0-45

ize that there is a greater future identity to be realized. At this time, many young people have visions that they are going to die about the age of 30. Esoterically, what they are experiencing from inside is the challenge to realize that a Christ body is in them and, yes, the past identity will be crucified in its favor, so that the true spiritual identity of the individual can live in the society-created vehicle of operation.

This period is quite scary for many individuals and yet when the quintile aspect begins to operate at about 24 years of age, personal creative techniques can relieve the pressure that came at the last quarter square. In fact at 24 to 25 years of age, when the last quarter sextile operates it is easy to be productive and even to forget that challenge from inside. But this is an illusion.

At the age of 26 years, the semi-square begins to operate and there is A MOBILIZATION FROM INSIDE, a severe challenge to act, mentally, ahead of time, on an identity that will be ready for restructuring into an instinctive new kind of self at the age of 30.

At the age of 27 years the semi-sextile begins to operate and there is a tremendous effort required to fuse the two bodies--the psychologically CONSCIOUS identity of the past and the YET INSECURE identity of the future. This Balsamic Phase of the Saturn cycle of position is the great "mutation" that is required to move from one kind of identity to another. At this age and the others up to 30, the young person begins to realize he is on his own, he is no longer a possession of his parents or his society, and he has a chance to become a real individual.

At the orb of conjunction at about 29 to 30 years, the new identity begins to want to live. The "crisis" that comes from this conjunction is merely the decision whether the old identity will give up gracefully and let the new one live, or whether, in the coming CRESCENT phase, at about 34 years old, the "past will hang on like a ghost and the whole process will fail."

Let's consider the second Saturn cycle of position by transit.

DEFINE YOUR SEPARATENESS, REDEFINE YOUR "IDENTITY" (The individual is about 28 to 30 years of age and Saturn has re-entered the sign it occupied at his birth). It is time now to understand that you are capable of being an individual on your own. Society has provided you with a psychological vehicle of identity which you can now abandon in favor of an instinctive one that wants to come up from inside. Yes, the "you" that everyone previously knew can die, but only psychically, at this time. You have got to begin to realize your own individual potential and start acting it out. This individuality inside, and its real originality lies in Uranus' position at birth, can now take over the vehicle your society has created for it to operate in. If this period is a real "crisis," it is only because society has never taught its children that this IS THE REAL TIME OF ADULTHOOD. This is the time when one actually GOES ON HIS OWN. If an individual is 30 years of age and still living at home and under his parents' wings, there is something wrong. For this is the time when a whole new world can open up to him. Many people change entirely, from what they have "apparently been" before, at this time. They have to decide at this point a very simple thing: AM I GOING TO BE MYSELF OR WHAT EVERYONE ELSE WANTS ME TO BE, or what it may have been necessary to be to get this far?

THE COMMON MANIFESTATION is a crisis, an unbelievable feeling that everything that has gone on so far has been empty and meaningless in the light of what's beginning to surface. Some people actually contemplate suicide. Others come to that point where they realize that what they had been projecting as a life course wasn't "really them" at all. A lot of marriages break up because they were geared to some social image the parents wanted or that the youngsters succumbed to. Many individuals drop a whole life course and adopt another. Yes, something DOES die. What you were, before, in other people's ideas, is no longer effective. Unless your life projection was geared to your actual potential (your birth chart potential), rather than what you or your parents dreamed up as socially good, it can seem like the world is falling apart. Many individuals' lives ARE shattered at this point BECAUSE NOTHING PREPARED THEM FOR THE FACT THAT THIS IS THE ACTUAL TIME OF INDEPENDENCE IN

In this Saturn cycle, I will describe the phases and aspects in detail, because they are so seldom talked about and so seldom illustrated when THEY ARE OPERATING whether we are aware of them or not.

PUT YOUR NEW SELF TOGETHER WITH THE SHREDS OF THE OLD AND MOVE FORWARD (Saturn is one sign beyond its birth position and making the semi-sextile for the second time to its birth position). It is time now to look at the old identity, see what was worthwhile in it, and incorporate it into the instinctive new self that is trying to operate in you. It may take enormous effort--you are really combining two polarities of being--but the period ahead of you will make it worthwhile. This is where you DO have to work to put your old self and your new self together. But the new self is instinctive and it's ready to go. Accept the irritation of the loss of the old and incorporate its best features into this new you.

THE USUAL MANIFESTATION is that one is bewildered. He knows that "something in him has died." Where is he going? How is he going to face life with this new surge of "being somehow completely different than I was before?" But if those who will live it will look at it, they will see this: There is freedom here. There is complete freedom if one wants it. But why completely abandon something it took 30 years to build. Many individuals go off on a complete binge at this point, trouncing the old self, refusing to realize that it has many virtues which can be incorporated into this new drive to be an individual. They cut the polarities apart rather than fusing them and will come to a time when it will be easy to regret it. I have a poignant wish, whenever I see a person in the first flush of his new self after the 28-to-30 years old "identity crisis," to tell him, "Don't forget that what you WERE is still there to be used. You don't have to entirely destroy it. Even if you didn't realize it, something inside did. Many of the things you learned that you now see as futile can be incorporated into a greater self. Those skills you learned, which you now see as hopeless to your task, can be powerful for the identity still to find its complete activity. Yes, you are free. But don't waste the past. Look at it again. Just don't give it the same names. Don't you see that THERE'S SOMETHING BETTER YOU COULD MAKE OUT OF ALL THOSE SKILLS, ALL THOSE EXPERIENCES? Don't simply abandon them. Try to understand how you can USE them."

IN THIS NEW PHASE, the new identity instinctively pushes forward unless everything in the person refuses to let it live. It operates spontaneously and it was meant to. Things shouldn't really be thought out. They should be lived out. There is a kind of new "charisma" the individual can manifest through this new "identity" he is living out, or actually that is living out through his old vehicle of consciousness. If one wants to change his "name," this is the time to do it. And, instinctively, usually, the new and more fitting name is there. If it isn't a name, often, it's a social function--a new way of surviving in society, a new approach to life in all ways. Yes, it's a very good time to break away from a past line of endeavor and plunge into a new one. But, DURING THE IDENTITY CRISIS, between the ages of 26 and 30 when it was just setting in, ONE SHOULD HAVE THOUGHT OUT CONSCIOUSLY what it will now be easy to project instinctively. We can only hope that one did that. For the next aspect will be a severe test if one didn't.

MOVE FORWARD COMBATIVELY (Saturn is making the semi-square, by sign or aspect to its birth position), MARSHALL YOUR RESOURCES AND MOVE EFFECTIVE-LY OUT OF THE PAST. This is the time when the "new" you triumphs over the "old" you. It is when it is most instinctively effective in BECOMING ITSELF. This may not be without pressure from parents and society, but it is time to accept that pressure and move through it. It is time to become, in reality, what you dreamed about during the 26 to 30 age period. You ARE something new. You cannot go back to the past. You must realize that instinctively and move onward. You must now put your new "name," or your new "identity," into action so that it is noticed as the real you. This can be a struggle at first, but it will grow stronger and stronger over the next five years.

FQ 90-135

THE USUAL MANIFESTATION is that the individual feels "the past is trying to hang on in a death grip." If he has left a job, left a marriage partner, left his carefully planned future, parents, old friends and even social acquaintances seem to "haunt" him. They don't want to accept the new identity. They don't want him to be "himself." It was so comfortable the other way. He must mobilize all his resources in this new identity and activity and NOT LET THE PAST CLING TO HIM. It is often best for the individual to put some distance between himself and past associates at this point, particularly in our neurotic modern society. Many SHOULD get away from home and don't, and they ARE haunted and almost killed off in the new self. The feeling that "I represent the new and cannot go back to the past" is a good one. It should be encouraged. The past can be USED in many ways, but it cannot be lived again. Many have fond remembrances of what they were about 26 to 30 and yearn for it again. They have crossed a bridge and there is no going back, except to disaster. Yet many choose to, and many fledgling lives of individuality are killed right here. Then the psychological body that could have been withers and dies and at about age 42 one realizes that without having done something that really fitted one's actual potential, life was not worth much.

THIS IS THE CRESCENT PHASE of the Saturn cycle of position. It is most critical that mobilization take place and the individual move forward on his new realizations. Even if it is a struggle at first, around the age of 34 to 35, that struggle can become very productive around the 35th year and can become highly creative about the 36th year when the sextile and quintile aspect of this phase are operating. It's a time to break from the past, and it probably WILL try to cling, but ghosts are only effective if we allow them to be. ONE MUST REPOLARIZE HIS EXISTENCE HERE. Once he does so, the forward movement will not be stopped. If he does not, that age of 42 can become a real hell. This is the period of life when most creative individuals are actively involved in their great creative works which bring them to prominence at about age 40 through 42 when the trine and biquintile of the first quarter phase of the Saturn cycle of position are operating. Yes, this crescent phase IS a struggle, but one that will certainly prove worth it when he later watches those, who failed in it, fall apart at the male and female "menopause."

MEET CRISIS AND PLUNGE ON; YOU ARE ABOUT TO OPERATE EFFECTIVELY AND THIS "CRISIS" CAN BE CREATIVE (Saturn is moving in sign, or aspect, square to its birth position). It is time for you to challenge your surroundings with this new "you." It is time to move out there and clear away the activities and ideas that thwart your new self from self-expression. There will probably be a lot of talk and a lot of action surrounding your instinctive putting of your new self forward. This is a creative crisis. Accept it. Challenge yourself and, if you really have something to offer, the ideas that surround you. This is an active period for most creative individuals. It is not always pleasant because they have to plunge into critical situations and manage them into something productive. You learn "management of yourself," under this aspect, too. Ideas and activities that are frustrating to your self-expression must either be got out of the way or put into proper perspective. This is a time when you will be irritated by reactions but you will probably irritate others, too, and this is creatively good even if it doesn't look "good" to the desired placidity that most people imagine for themselves. This is the peak of creative bursts of activity. They're instinctive. If you allow them to happen, they will sometimes frighten you, but they will also make possible what is just ahead--the Saturn trine and quintile at 39 to 40 years of age. At that point, the crises you handled here will turn into easily flowing creative energy and personally creative techniques. If you want to be recognized in any way, it will be "easy" then BECAUSE of what you faced as a kind of instinctive crisis here.

THE USUAL MANIFESTATION is that individuals break down under the challenge of their surroundings. They have been projecting a new identity and suddenly there is opposition to it. Suddenly, obstacles arise to it. Suddenly, others become combative physically or intellectually. This is good, really, for anything creative, but it is frightening to the psyche that wants things to be "easy." Well, in any cycle of aspects, a "trine" always follows after a "square." An easy flow of energy, in other words, comes out of a crisis creatively faced. But we are not often taught that, in a society that seeks complete "security," and so this period looks "bad" to many individuals engaged in it. They feel frustrated by their surroundings, handicapped by the energy coming at them. Some "fail" after having moved this far forward. It doesn't have to be that way. The "failure" WILL lead to an "easy out" at the trine aspect, but IT COULD lead to "a creative outpouring of energy" if the crisis is faced and managed, even if one doesn't know how. Sometimes he gets a mere glimmer of what's ahead. It isn't clearly outlined but even its vagueness seems worth fighting for. And this is true. Its outlines will become clearer and clearer, but here is where the movement is tested.

THIS FIRST QUARTER PHASE of Saturn's transitting cycle to its birth position is one of excitement and activity if one can take it. Life can seem vivid. The individual will instinctively be combative in putting forth himself or his ideas. And this is actually constructive. Or will be. The square, which produces many crises, for the emerging new personality to handle, turns into the trine which is a creative flow of energy. In other words, creation follows crisis. The world is challenging us not only to BE a new self, but to EXPRESS A NEW SELF into the surroundings. There is an instinctive urge to clear everything out of the way that impedes or hampers one's expression, that shackles his creative energy. There's a dim vision of something ahead that cannot yet be clearly visualized but it must be moved toward. Yes, it must. The individual will perfect his techniques and prove his social worth later under the Gibbous phase of this Saturn cycle, but now HE MUST PLUNGE IN AND FACE WHAT THERE IS TO BE FACED. He must "manage" crisis by learning through it. He's no technician yet in his activities, but he soon will be if he moves through this period with energy.

**GI
135-180**

 PERFECT YOUR TECHNIQUES: PREPARE TO GO OUTSIDE YOURSELF AND PER-SONAL INVOLVEMENT (Saturn is nearly five signs beyond its birth position and the age reached is about 40 to 41 years). If the creative potential has been allowed to grow, it is time now to analyze what you have been doing and become aware of where it's leading. You must, at this point, perfect the techniques you have been using--exclude from them all that are superfluous to what you are doing. It is time, too, to challenge your surroundings and have them answer some questions for you. It may be, at this time, that the surroundings will challenge you to question exactly what it is you are doing, where it is leading and of what worth this is to others as well as yourself. You have come through a long period of acting out, instinctively, a new identity that began at the last Saturn conjunction. This is a period of adjustment. It will soon become clear, if it is not already so, that the instinctive action of this cycle is about over. If you wish to carry the activity much farther, it will be as a result of some meaningful realization that comes at the Saturn opposition. Before that, however, at about the ages 41 to 42, you can USE the personally creative techniques you have adopted to produce very strongly in one last, perhaps long burst of activity, that is DEPENDENT upon your ability to use the production techniques you have adopted (this is when the biquintile aspect operates). Shortly after that, at age 42 to 43, there will come a tendency to veer off course from the goals you may have established some-what insecurely as this analysis, and perfection of technique, cycle began at age 40 to 41. Whatever else happens, however, THERE IS A DAWNING REALIZATION THAT SOMETHING NEW IS ABOUT TO COME TO CONSCIOUSNESS and if you polish your personal techniques for handling personal problems, NOW, there will be little problem with them when the realization actually comes and lifts you into a new world of con-sciousness. Watch carefully, the period 42 to 43 years of age. It will require quite a bit of discipline to keep from veering off course, to keep from avoiding the realization state that is due to arrive.

THE USUAL MANIFESTATION of this period is that the individual begins meeting challenges again from his surroundings. Personal doubts set in about what he has been doing. He wonders if it has all been worth anything. He wants to know HOW it has been operating and WHY it has been operating--this movement forward on the basis of a new identity since the Saturn conjunction with its birth position. The worst manifesta-tion is a kind of noisy confusion about the individual's own worth. Why am I doing all these things? What in the world has it been for? Where have I gone wrong? Questions

saturn in its main cycle

like that, virtually screamed out to the surroundings, indicate that when the age of 42 to 43 arrives, the individual may be in even more confusion. And when the opposition comes, he can feel that everything is falling apart on him. The questions need to be asked, the situations that have developed from the conjunction need to be analyzed, BUT THE PURPOSE OF THIS is not to attain confusion, but to attain personal efficiency of operation so one can go BEYOND intense personal involvement. If the trine aspect, at 39 to 40 years of age was a mere relief from crisis, a kind of coasting away from challenges presented at 37 to 38 years of age, there is even worse to come. This is a critical state of psychological adjustment. The individual who is operating creatively will use it to perfect his techniques so he can go beyond them-- so he can HAVE THEM OPERATING and then give them some meaningful purpose or content after the opposition to come at 44 to 45 years of age. The individual who is not will probably start feeling that his world is falling apart. After one severe crisis at about age 37, this age 41 is bringing another one and then the age 43 is bringing an even more irritating one. The individual who has not adopted any individual identity since the age of 30 will feel, often, that he is falling apart physically at this point. Of course, he is. Physically vitality has reached its peak. And this will become extremely obvious at about age 44 to 45. If there's nothing else there to operate, it will be quite disillusioning.

THIS GIBBOUS PHASE of Saturn's transitting cycle to its birth position is an extremely critical one for the "typical cultural type." It is the beginning of the failing of his physical and emotional vitality. For the creative type, it is not that in any way. In fact, it is one of the peaks of instinctive productive power before one consciously uses that power in the late 40's. The creative type will realize that physical vitality is not going to carry him on forever and he will, during the Gibbous phase of this cycle, perfect his techniques of production, analyze his activities until he feels they are of social worth, and prepare for the new consciousness he will come into at the time when physical vitality ebbs and spiritual, or individual, vitality takes over. This is a sad period for most individuals who have built their lives around sexual and cultural activities. The "menopause," for both men and women sets in. And if they have nothing beyond their personal attractiveness to lead them beyond this point, the rude awakening begins to set in. For the creative man, whose children is in his works, this is a peak period of production and realization that he can now go out of exclusive personal involvement and see his works move out to where they are having an effect not only on him while he is producing them but on others to whom the spirit of him speaks through them. Individuals who have built their lives around raising children now begin to see the fruition of that, in one way or another. If it is well-handled, they now have the opportunity to go on to some other kind of involvement; if it has not, the realization sets in.

age 45

FU 180-135

LOOK NOW FOR A REALIZATION, A MEANING, A CONTENT, A PURPOSE FOR THE FUTURE OPERATION OF YOUR INDIVIDUAL SELF (Saturn is opposing its birth position--the age is about 44 to 45 years). Up to this time, you have been operating instinctively as an individual. You must now become aware of a further purpose for this operation. Mere activity for activity's sake, cannot go beyond this point. You must incorporate some new goal. What you have done, for 15 years, is build a personal identity that now must have some social goal--some meaning in the eyes of others, in their lives, as well as in your own. It is time for a major realization. If you are the creative individual, you have reached the peak of your individual creative output. There will be some new dimension now added to it, or it will seem futile to continue along the same instinctive lines of endeavor. If you are ever going to have a major illumination, it will be now. Let what is outside your personal realm of awareness enter at this point. It will completely transform your activity. That doesn't mean it has to cease; it merely means it must have a new purpose, a new goal, a larger content, a greater meaning, a larger sense of perspective. Once you have reached this realization, you will "move on from what you have been doing" at the age of 46 to 47 and achieve a greater kind of "personal technique of creative functioning" at about 47 to 48 years, just before you reach the peak of your ability to spread the new idea, the new realization, the new content of your creative production in the next phase of Saturn's cycle.

THE USUAL MANIFESTATION of this opposition of Saturn to its own birth position is a complete breakdown of activity. The individual begins to feel that everything has been futile. His life is empty. He has "gotten nowhere" and now even his physical vitality is beginning to fail him. This Saturn opposition, the second one in the lifetime, coincides with the first opposition of Uranus to its birth position and precedes the fourth conjunction of Jupiter with its birth position. The Uranus opposition is a challenge to become an individual if one has not already done so--to find something that is actually self-expressive and not merely a requirement of existence. The Saturn opposition is a signal that one cycle of individual expression has reached its peak and needs content, meaning, purpose or goal to move forward. The coming Jupiter conjunction is the indicator of a completely new forward movement socially and personally. If the individual has not been creative, or has not adopted an individuality that fits his potential before this time, it is likely to be a period of great disillusion. He realizes that half his life has passed AND WHAT HAS HE DONE WITH IT? For many this is a time of personal breakdown and futility. They realize they've only got so many years left and they become frantic to do something with them. It need not be that way.

THE FULL PHASE of the Saturn cycle of position to its own birth place is the peak period of the creative life. It is the time when an individual has been living creatively in instinctive ways and suddenly incorporates into his work some new goal, some new meaning or some new dimension. It can be a time of great illumination and great awareness before a cycle of spreading ideas begins. If it is not, then it is a frantic time to find some last-minute activity that can make the person feel his life has not been entirely futile. If it is the time of realization, then the ages 46 to 47, can be the moving away from the past activity of spontaneous production, into a period at 47 to 48 when personal creativity finds new techniques and moves toward a challenge of its surroundings with the spreading, or living out, of some great idea or activity.

age
49

DI
135-90

CHALLENGE YOUR SURROUNDINGS WITH WHAT YOU BELIEVE; CONVEY IT, LIVE IT OUT : THIS IS YOUR MOST CREATIVE PERIOD (Saturn forms the 135 degree aspect with its birth position--the age is 49 to 50). The individual who has made something of his life, who built an individual identity at 30 and lived it out instinctively until 44 to 45, then incorporated into that identity some new meaning, new goal, or new realization, is now ready to become a popularizer of what he believes, a conveyor of what has impressed him by experience, an individual living out, in word and deed, what he believes to be worth something not only to himself but to others as well. At 48 to 49 years of age, he can move into his surroundings and challenge them with this idea. If he successfully does this, the creative flow of the idea moves unimpeded from the age of 50 on to about 53 when he begins to go back into himself for an inner conversion. But here is where he reaches the period when everything he has done since the age of 30 becomes meaningful to him and to others as well. Most individuals who are doing something of value find that at the opposition they found some new realization that heightened their work and now it proliferates in shape, in content, in depth and this is something vivid that they seem to convey through their very presence. This is the real peak of the life of individuality and individual expression. What is produced now has the spark of conviction, almost a messianic quality.

THE USUAL MANIFESTATION is a feeling of utter hopelessness. There should have been something to live for but what was it? The individual feels he "wants" some idea to convey. Many fall prey to some other individual's idea and, finding that they had nothing to convey from their own experience, decide to convey something at least. Some people, who have found nothing to live for, become fanatics at this period-- joining some great religion, some great movement, some great fad, because that's all there is to make their lives vivid. They try to live through someone else. But the creative man does not have to do this--he has had his realization and his vividness is authentic, so authentic, in fact, that he often picks up those disillusioned I have mentioned as rapt devotees and fanatic followers. They become the dying vegetation of the "cultural mould" in which he plants his ideas, which will use their fading vitality to grow to life out of. For the individual who has found nothing but an idea to attach himself to, this is the waning hours of the individual life. From here on, society offers little but retirement and the slow movement toward the last hours.

**saturn
in
its
main
cycle**

age
53

LQ
90-45

THIS DISSEMINATING PHASE of the Saturn cycle of position is one of the most beautiful parts of the cycle of individual expression for the person who decided, at 30, to become an individual according to his own potential. It is here, usually, that he meets public recognition and finds himself vivid in the expression of what it was he came to convey or live out. For the individual who failed to be an individual there is little left to do but sacrifice oneself to someone else's ideal so that at least the vitality can be molded to some newer, fresher thing that could take life from one's own failures.

REACH INWARD NOW: A GREATER DESTINY IS WAITING TO BE MET (Saturn is making the last quarter square to its birth position--the age is about 52 to 53 years). This is the time for an inner conversion. It does not have to show on the surface at all, but it must be met inside, for the challenge comes from in there. There is an idea, a glimmer of the future, that waits to be met, even if you do not yet reveal this to anyone on the outside. But the challenge cannot really be ignored, for it will spring to life through you, in some way about seven years from this point. It is time to change directions mentally because YOU CHOOSE TO. You still retain all the competence you have had before this. The only difference is that now there is the call from inside to be recognized. What will most likely happen is that you will maintain the facade of what you have been doing--you can function consciously without much effort--but now you need to listen to the inner voice and get ready to live on its terms about seven years from now. This crisis will come from inside even though you ignore it, even though you don't show it outside. There's a very simple reason. The cycle of individual activity is about over on the individual-istic level and what's inside is ready to prepare you for what's ahead in another cycle.

THE USUAL MANIFESTATION is that the individual, at the peak of his competence and expression, begins to feel inner rumblings. He hides them, he tries to quell them, but they won't go away. There's a kind of divine discontent inside. One can keep his competent facade going, but it may be like living with an inner scream if he does not, to himself, acknowledge, that there is a greater presence inside to be realized. Most people go through this period, performing competently and then about 3 and a half years after it begins, start to do bewildering things or make bewildering pronouncements. Sometimes they start to take "inflexible stands based on principle," though they fail to explain the principle. They think they dare not, for what is really happening is that they are severely challenged from inside to "become a new person" and they will have to break this abruptly to those around them WHEN THEY FEEL THEY ARE READY. And, obviously, trying to ignore the whole thing, they know they are not ready.

THIS LAST QUARTER PHASE of Saturn's cycle of position IS THE CONVERSION POINT. One can choose, consciously, to break from the past cycle of activity. In that case, at about the age of 54 years there comes a personally creative time when this can be done intellectually--when one can begin to change his image even if he makes what some people do not understand as a complete change of "identity" inside. Then at the age of 54 to 55, when the last quarter sextile aspect operates, it is possible to go about this identity change productively with just a little conscious effort applied. Yes, this IS a changeover period. But it's a changeover in conscious-ness more than in action. That will come in the next step.

ADD UP THE PAST, DECIDE WHAT YOU WILL CHOOSE TOWARD THE FUTURE, AND BEGIN MOVING ON IT, EVEN IF THIS SEEMS PREMATURE (Saturn is making the last quarter semi-square to its birth position; the age is about 56 years). A cycle of individual activity, both instinctive and consciously motivated, has come to an end. What you are now is the result of that process. What do you feel you lack? What do you feel you want as a result of all the activity? Choose now, because in about three years' time, you will be involved, instinctively, in what you are consciously choosing now as desires and hopes. In fact, at this point, you prematurely begin the activities into which you will be plunged for the rest of your life. What you MUST do, if possible, is SHAPE THOSE ACTIVITIES NOW MENTALLY. Make choices about

THE USUAL MANIFESTATION is, that at the end of a long and bewildering life of futile activity, or activity that was geared to family or society's ideas, rather than one's own potential, the individual BEGINS TO YEARN FOR WHAT HE WAS NOT. He begins to long to be what he failed to be. He begins to add up all his liabilities and curse them. He begins to draw up all his desires and focus upon them. The one great mistake that most people make, is that they utterly curse all they have been. They imagine a completely new kind of existence, excluding all that they were. This can be called a "karmic" phase of the Saturn cycle. One's desires are at their peak, even if they have not previously been gratified. It IS a good time to ponder what could have been done better, but it is not a good time to burn down the house to get a spot off the wall. What people wish during this cycle, often manifests in the next Saturn cycle or one that will open a new life in another body. This is the age of retirement in the modern society and what one wishes for he can plunge into from here on because there's little else to do. If he never had any free time to devote to any one special thing, he may over-idealize that and plunge immediately and completely into it upon retirement. Only later does he realize this could have been thought out somewhat better. At any rate, this is a period when people who have been thwarted in becoming individuals often make the greatest mistake of all. They dream of freeing themselves from what they were and becoming all they weren't. And they often get their wish--which had nothing to do with their potential but with their wasted choices.

THIS BALSAMIC PHASE of the Saturn cycle of position is a critical state of existence again. It is the time when one moves from the cycle of individual expression to the cycle of spiritual or socially valuable expression. In other words, he has lived out his own individual name; now he can live out the name of his beliefs or his social awarenesses. What he did before for himself, he can now do for the whole to which he imagines himself belonging--whether this is family, society, religion or mankind, as he envisions it. The first premature steps are plunged into here, consciously, and when the next cycle begins they are plunged into wholly and instinctively. One WISHES THEM INTO BEING CONSCIOUSLY HERE. At the age of about 57 years, when the last semi-sextile of the cycle operates, he can, with tremendous effort, put his desires together with the vehicle of consciousness he has to operate with at this point, and begin the activity consciously so that when the next Saturn return begins the activity is not a crisis, but an extension, instinctively, of what was begun here in consciousness. Whatever else happens, there is the great realization that what one now is, is the end product of the whole previous 30-year cycle. And he stands now at the threshold of moving up to the power bestowed in him at birth by Neptune's position or at the threshold of a kind of dimming age of slow dissolution. The choice of what it will be is up to him and the power of conscious image-making he has evolved in the first 58 to 60 years of his life.

At this point, with the next conjunction of Saturn to its own birth position, the cycle repeats itself, with the same basic purposes (phases) and accentuations of purpose (aspects within the phases) except that THIS TIME THE NEW IDENTITY IS NOT ADOPTED FOR PURPOSES OF SELF-EXPRESSION BUT FOR THE REALIZATION OF YOURSELF THAT GOES BEYOND SELF-EXPRESSION--what you are in the light of your faith, your god, your fellow men and humanity; in other words, what you are as a PART OF A GREATER WHOLE THAN YOUR INDIVIDUAL SELF.

Let's take a brief review of the cycle we have just discussed and see the essential nature of it.

At about the ages 28 to 30, we have the transitting Saturn return to its birth position. This is when we TRY TO DEFINE OUR REAL SEPARATENESS AND REDEFINE OUR IDENTITY IN SOCIAL TERMS. The conjunction opens the New Phase of action which is for the purpose of INSTINCTIVE PROJECTION of this new self. Within the phase operates the semi-sextile which is for the purpose of "merging two polarities-- the old vehicle and the new consciousness."

saturn in its main cycle

age 56

BA 45-0

again:

29

saturn in its main cycle

At about the ages of 34 to 35 Saturn makes the semi-square aspect to its birth position and opens the Crescent Phase of activity whose purpose is a STRUGGLE FORWARD, OUT OF THE PAST, WITH THIS NEW IDENTITY. Within this phase operates the semi-square, the challenge to action; the sextile around 35 years of age, which represents an accentuation on production with a little effort; and then the quintile, at about 36, which represents personal creativity in that process of production.

At about 37 to 38 years of age, Saturn squares, by transit, its birth position opening the First Quarter phase of activity whose purpose is A CREATIVE CRISIS TO PLUNGE THE PERSONALITY INTO ACTIVITY IN ITS SURROUNDINGS. Within this phase operates the accentuated aspect of the square, to produce crisis and challenge; and then, at about age 39 to 40, the trine aspect, which represents the accentuation of creation as the result of challenge and crisis.

At about the age of 40 to 41 years, comes Saturn's 135-degree aspect to its birth position opening up the Gibbous phase of activity whose purpose is A PERFECTION OF PERSONAL TECHNIQUES OF OPERATION. This starts with the sesquiquadrate (135 degrees) which accentuates challenge to or from the surroundings to get the process started; then the biquintile (144 degrees) to call out the individual's ability to use personally creative techniques in this challenge; and then the quincunx (150 degrees) just a few years before operation, to make the individual examine the fact that he has a tendency to veer off course from his goal, which is just ahead.

Finally, at the ages of 44 to 45 years, Saturn makes its opposition to its birth position and the Full phase opens. The purpose of this phase of activity is to SEEK REALIZATION OR CONTENT OR MEANING FOR THE FUTURE OPERATION OF SELF. Within this phase operates the 180 degree aspect which forces the individual to realize that he can no longer proceed on instinct. He must now be conscious before he acts. Then operates the quincunx, which moves the process away from the realization and toward another biquintile, or another application of personal techniques to move toward the next phase of activity.

At ages 49 to 50, another sesquiquadrate operates, opening the Disseminating phase whose purpose is to CHALLENGE THE SURROUNDINGS WITH WHAT YOUR AWARE SELF NOW KNOWS--TO LIVE THIS OUT, TO CONVEY IT, INTO THE SURROUNDINGS. Within this phase operates the 135-degree "challenge" accentuation and then, after the challenge, the 120-degree aspect of a "creative flow of energy that comes as the living creation after the living crisis, consciously precipitated."

At about ages 52 to 53, there begins operating the second square of Saturn to its birth position, opening the Last Quarter phase of activity whose purpose is a REORIENTATION OF CONSCIOUSNESS AND, IF POSSIBLE, A BREAK, IN AWARENESS, FROM THE PAST CYCLE OF ACTIVITY. First there is the "crisis inside," precipitated by the accentuation of the square aspect and then, as the sextile aspect forms, the ability "to take productive action after personally creative activity (the 72-degree aspect which preceded it) as a result of the crisis inside (the square)."

At about age 56, Saturn makes its last semi-square aspect of the cycle, opening up the Balsamic phase of activity whose purpose is A CONSCIOUS MUTATION OR BREAK FROM THE PAST AND MOVEMENT TOWARD THE FUTURE. Within this phase operates the semi-square which creates the "mobilization inward," and then the semi-sextile, which accentuates the need to "merge the polarities--the consciousness of now with the prospect of the future." And then we move toward the next cycle of activity ushered in, instinctively, by the conjunction which again recreates the identity, or structural side of consciousness, at another higher level of awareness--the Neptunian level of being part of a greater whole than individual self.

What is interesting about reviewing this cycle is that if we watch what people actually do in life, as it moves along, we will find them reacting strongly to the conjunction, the first quarter square, the opposition and the last quarter square--the most "potent" or energy-releasing "aspects" of the cycle of aspects.

But what must be done, eventually, is to get individuals to realize that THESE ASPECTS DO NOT OPERATE SEPARATELY, NOR HAPHAZARDLY--THEY FOLLOW ONE ANOTHER IN KNOWABLE ORDER. There is activity before them and after them and there is a CONTINUING CYCLE OF ACTIVITY even if, because of the "softer," or "form-building" aspects, the conjunction, square and opposition stand out.

They are simply DYNAMIC RELEASES of energy WITHIN a total cyclic flow of energy.

Most people never forget the conjunction, especially if they are not prepared for it. They battle their way instinctively through the first quarter square. They tend to fall apart at the opposition and they try to hide, or evade, the inner crisis at the last quarter square. If they could see the whole cycle and realize what is happening, there would be no great worry at all.

And what is this all doing, as far as the "houses" and "quadrants" and "signs" are concerned? Well, when we are looking at a birth chart--and considering the Saturn cycle of position to its birth position--we must look to the sign CAPRICORN. Wherever this falls, in the birth chart, by house and by quadrant, is the AREA OF REALIZATION AND THE FIELD OF ACTIVITIES where the "manifestation" of this cycle of identity change will want to release itself in activity and realization.

When we have located the house that has Capricorn on it, we should consider WHERE SATURN WILL BE IN THE CYCLE OF POSITION WHEN IT TRANSITS THAT HOUSE AND SIGN. What phase will it be in, in its cycle of position? And what aspect will it be making, if any?

Define the ability to adjust to what is beyond involvement with others & the community.

Define the ability to express through others and the community.

Define the role you hold in the larger community.

Define the ability to extend awareness outward.

Define the substance of involvement with others.

Define awareness of, and involvement with, others.

10   9

11   8

12   7

IV QUADRANT 4; Growth in influence among others.

III QUADRANT 3: Growth in awareness of, and functioning with, others.

1

I QUADRANT 1: Growth in self-awareness and projection.

II QUADRANT 2: Growth in self-expression.

2   6

3   4   5

Define self-awareness and projection of it.

Define the substance of self-awareness.

Define the ability to extend self into surroundings.

Define the ability to focalize self-awareness & projection.

Define the ability to achieve self-expression.

Define the ability to adjust to what's outside self.

**the
vital
sun
cycle**

**NW
0-45**

**CR
45-90**

DEFINE YOUR BASIC PURPOSE, DISCIPLINE YOUR VITAL ENERGIES (Saturn
is transitting the sign in which your Sun is located at birth--the pattern emerges as
soon as it enters the sign, reaches intensity when it reaches the Sun's degree position in the sign). It's time to decide what your real purposes are and where they
are leading you. The Sun, by house position at birth, indicates what field of activities your conscious purpose is centered upon. By sign position, it indicates the general approach you take to these activities. Now the time has come to define that approach
and KNOW what your goals and purpose are centered upon. At the conjunction, the
process of realizing your purpose begins. It can reach manifestation, in activity
and attitude, when Saturn transits the field of activities in your chart that bears the
Zodiacal sign Leo. But here is where it all begins. You may have come to the end
of a long process of activity which now reaches a successful climax BECAUSE YOU
HAVE WORKED, FOR AT LEAST SEVEN YEARS, TO THAT END. Or you may begin
to realize that activities, in which you've been engaged, haphazardly for a long time,
DO NOT FIT YOUR BASIC PURPOSE and it is time to consider WHAT WILL FIT IT.
AND HEAD IN THAT DIRECTION. Whatever the case, you must manage, now, your
vital energies and set them on the track that DOES fit your basic purpose. What
house of the birth chart is this happening in? What quadrant? What sign? Go back
and read the interpretations for that quadrant, house and sign, and combine them with
what's called for here--a definition of your real purpose, a disciplining of your vital
energies so they are geared to it. What happens now can manifest in another way,
in other activities and other attitudes, when Saturn, by transit, reaches the sector
of your birth chart marked by the sign Leo.

THE USUAL MANIFESTATION is that the individual, confused for some time in what
he has been doing, finally feels that he has been on the wrong track for some time.
He feels frustrated in his goals, defeated in his purposes, and whatever he has been
engaged in comes to a head. And falls apart. But this is ONLY true if he has been
moving haphazardly. If he knows what he's doing, if he has worked on it step by
step for some time, this can be the climax of a successful operation--successful because the person himself MADE IT SO. Many people, at the time of this conjunction,
come to the end of one line of activities--feeling they have been on the wrong track
for a long time--and begin moving on another. Many, also, build to a successful con-
clusion--usually under pressure and added responsibility--what they have worked toward for a long time. If one is living out his basic purpose, he has nothing to worry
about. But he must accept added responsibility and he usually has to work under pressure. Sometimes the individual feels his vitality is at a low ebb. This is only because
he HAS NOT disciplined his energies to the tasks at hand. He must now do that. He
must economize on his energy so that he is not wasting it. It must be geared to his
basic goals and purposes. Any other use of it is a waste. The Air Signs and the Fire
Signs of the Zodiac usually groan, strain and scream under this transit. The Water
Signs and the Earth Signs seem to take it with less commotion, but they feel the pressure, nevertheless. This is one of the times in life when AN INDIVIDUAL BECOMES
RESPONSIBLE WHETHER HE LIKES IT OR NOT, because his purpose is being tested
and his vitality is coming under discipline.

THE NEW PHASE -- (from the conjunction to about 5 years after) -- MOVE SPON-
TANEOUSLY TO YOUR BASIC PURPOSE. About 2 to 3 years after the conjunction you
must merge the relics of your past activities with this newly realized purpose. You
must put the shards of the past together with what you now see as the real task ahead
and move spontaneously toward it. If you don't, you are merely groaning through a
task which seems to have come upon you and which you will be able to avoid handily
(by plunging back into haphazard and directionless activity) about 3 years after the conjunction. What ARE you doing and why? Can you accept the responsibility and reality
of HAVING a basic purpose in life and acting it out? There's no better time than now
to realize this and begin moving forward, SLOWLY BUT SURELY, upon it.

THE CRESCENT PHASE (from 4 to 5 years after conjunction to about 7 to 8 years
after) -- STRUGGLE FORWARD WITH YOUR ESSENTIAL GOALS AND DON'T LET
THE PAST TRAP YOU. There's likely to be activity in your surroundings that challenges what you have established as your goals. Old friends and old ideas will try to
draw you back into the habits of the past. You have learned to be responsible and

after the conjunction, you will find that you only have to put a little effort into what you're doing now to make it PRODUCTIVE. About 5 to 6 years after the conjunction, you will notice, if you are really in a newly defined activity that fits your basic purposes, that your own personal creativity is coming into play in what you're doing. This SHOULD happen now because just ahead there is a challenge and a crisis and your ability to be productive and creative will be tested again.

THE FIRST QUARTER PHASE (About 7 to 8 years after conjunction up to 10 to 11 years after) -- FACE CRISIS, ACCEPT CHALLENGES: MOVE FORWARD COMBAT-IVELY, EITHER IN MIND OR ACTIVITY AND LEARN TO MANAGE THE ACTIONS YOU ARE INSTINCTIVELY SETTING IN MOTION. You have moved away from an old line of activity that came to a head, or an end, at the Saturn conjunction with your birth Sun's position. Now, you must move out into your surroundings with your new goal and direction and challenge the things that could frustrate that goal and direction from being expressed. Your vitality may plunge you into crises, but learn to plunge into them and manage them as best you can. Accept challenges. You are on your way and these challenges are an indication of it. At about 9 to 10 years after the conjunction you will find that these challenges and crises have led you into a highly creative period of activity. If you met them and managed them, the movement for several years will be easy. You SHOULD be creative, now, in what you're doing because you learned to create out of crisis and challenge. You're on your way.

THE GIBBOUS PHASE (About 11 years after the conjunction to about 14 or 15 years after) -- ANALYZE WHAT YOU'RE DOING. PERFECT YOUR TECHNIQUES. MAKE YOURSELF AN EFFICIENTLY OPERATING INDIVIDUAL. You can check your growth now against your surroundings. You can question the processes in which you've been involved. You should learn to hone down your techniques so you are not wasting energy in what you're doing. You should establish routines for making yourself efficiently productive. If you've got something to learn, spend a period of apprenticeship now learning it. About 12 years after the conjunction, you will be able to apply these personally creative techniques to all you're doing. About 12 to 13 years after the con-junction you will find you have the irritating habit of veering off course from what you've set as a goal. This veering off, sometimes, is because you've momentarily become absorbed in the techniques so much you've forgotten WHAT THEY ARE FOR. Check that. What's the real goal? You're just about to realize it consciously as you never have before. You acted spontaneously and instinctively up to this point. That was the right thing to do. You're about to arrive somewhere and you'll have to have a REASON AND A PURPOSE for acting. That's why you're learning to handle things so well technically. The emphasis will soon go off activity onto meaning. And you'll want to be able to operate effectively without much thought ABOUT THE DETAILS of operating, when the time for thought comes.

THE FULL PHASE (from the opposition to about 3 to 4 years after it) -- LOOK OUTSIDE WHAT YOU'VE BEEN DOING. HOW CAN YOUR ACTIVITY HAVE MORE MEANING, DEEPER CONTENT? WHAT COULD YOU INCORPORATE INTO IT THAT YOU HAVEN'T YET CONSIDERED? This is a climax period. You've come a long way. You've acted instinctively on some major goal. You've perfected your ability to operate within that goal. Now, you must put some CONSCIOUS CONTENT AND MEAN-ING INTO WHAT YOU'RE DOING. Emphasis goes off the energy you put into activity; and ONTO the meaning and purpose you put into the activity. You may want to change what you have been doing, alter it slightly to fit some new realization you have achiev-ed. This is an excellent urge. Follow it. Your basic purposes are being challenged now by the established ways of doing things. You must INTEGRATE the two. In other words, what you've been doing must have some CONSCIOUS RELEVANCE to what's outside you and around you. It must be of social worth as well as personal worth. Many people find this a time when they gain a major illumination about how the things they've been doing can fit into greater goals and greater purposes than mere personal satisfaction. If they don't, they find the activities falling apart because they aren't as acceptable as they once were. This is true BECAUSE THEY LACK PURPOSE IN THE EYES OF OTHERS. That's a major consideration now, because what is ahead is a popularizing, or living out in word and deed, what you have learned to be worth-while during the past 15 years. If anyone's going to accept it, it has to be of some worth to him, too. If you're terribly frustrated during this period, it's

the vital sun cycle

FQ 90-135

GI 135-180

FU 180-135

the vital sun cycle

DI

135-90

LQ

90-45

BA

45-0

because the world is demanding an answer from you. You'd better know what you're doing, why it has meaning and you'd better get ready to EXPLAIN IT CONSCIOUSLY. About a year after the opposition you should have realized what you can do to make your activities more meaningful and more geared to your surroundings. When this happens you can move away from what you've learned and begin applying a LARGER KIND of personal creativity and techniques of creative productivity to what you're doing. This happens about 2 years after the opposition and leads to the next step, the most important step of all--because it is the ACTUAL GOAL OF EVERYTHING THAT HAS BEEN HAPPENING FOR THE PAST 16 YEARS.

THE DISSEMINATING PHASE (About 3 to 4 years after the opposition to about 8 years after) -- ACT OUT WHAT YOU BELIEVE, PUT YOURSELF TRULY INTO YOUR ACTIVITIES AND SHOW OTHERS HOW THEY HAVE MEANING FOR THEM AS WELL AS FOR YOU. DRAMATIZE YOUR GOALS IN EFFECTIVE WAYS. You can now challenge your surroundings with the worth and meaning of your purpose and activities by living them out vividly. Your power to communicate the worth of your goals is at a peak. You can become a popularizer of some idea or activity in WHAT-EVER you're doing. Life should seem full and vivid. This is a peak of your personal vitality cycle. And it is there because, at the opposition, you integrated your purposes with the conditions of your surroundings and the needs of the world outside yourself. About 6 years after the opposition you will find yourself consciously creative, easily flowing to the activity you have meant to live out and dramatize. This is a period when you can get peak recognition for the fact that you HAD a basic purpose in life and you lived it out--no matter how small or how large it is. You will probably find people listening to you because you are conveying something of worth to them. And you BELIEVE in what you're doing or what you're thinking because it comes as the result of believing in things that life has impressed you are real and worthy. What you are doing now, you came into this life to do. And if that isn't true, you're bound to be frustrated at this period and running around frantically TRYING TO FIND SOMETHING YOU CAN PUT YOUR ENERGY INTO. If that's the case, you'll have to work fast because there's another challenge ahead.

THE LAST QUARTER PHASE (About 8 to 9 years after the opposition) -- SEARCH INSIDE: WHAT IS SOMETHING IN THERE TRYING TO TELL YOU? IT'S TIME FOR A REORIENTATION OF SPIRIT. You should be exceptionally competent, now, in anything you're doing. But there's a voice inside that is starting to haunt you. It is saying, "Look to the long range ahead. Start preparing mentally, now, to move to a new goal about seven years from now. What you dream now is important. It can materialize later." This can seem like a crisis, inside, really. While you're excep-tionally competent at what you're doing, the LIFE, the SPIRIT, the MEANING is starting to fade from it. That's because SOMETHING WAS ACCOMPLISHED THROUGH IT. And it's time to get ready for a new cycle of accomplishment, at least mentally. If you have a feeling you want to "change your image," you're on the right track. You will go inside yourself now and consider it and in about 4 years' time you will be ready to accomplish it on the outside. About 10 years after the opposition you will have the ability to put creative ability into changing your image and your goal. About 10 to 11 years after the opposition, you will be able to make this inner change produc-tively with just a little effort.

THE BALSAMIC PHASE (About 11 to 12 years after the opposition up to the next conjunction of Saturn with the birth Sun's position) -- PREPARE FOR THE FUTURE. REORIENT YOURSELF SO YOU CAN BEGIN TO ACT UPON WHAT YOU'RE DREAM-ING. Add up everything you've done since the last Saturn conjunction with your birth Sun's position. Are you satisfied with it? What could you have done better? What could you BE, as a person, that would have allowed you to function better in your goals and purposes? Decide now, because in about 3 to 4 years' time, everything you have worked on will either climax or come to a dead end. If you're thinking of some new goal, some new activation of basic purpose, you're on the right track. At about the 13th year after the opposition you will be able to merge the shell of the old activity cycle with the impulse of the new one you have dreamed and felt. You will be able to act out some things slightly ahead of their time. You will be able to plunge consciously into the new cycle of activity, but you won't be able to live it out spontaneously until the conjunction. Consider everything now that must be done to mentally prepare.

In the foregoing interpretations, it may have seemed to the intelligent reader that what was called for in the Saturn transit to its birth position was somewhat similar to what was called for in the Saturn transit to the birth position of the Sun.

And this is quite true.

One of our great problems, in understanding ourselves, is that both psychology and astrology are new to the mass intellectual definitions we have learned of what a human being is and how he operates.

Most people do not know how to distinguish their "identity," for instance, from their "fundamental purpose." And yet there is a distinguishing feature between them. Unless, of course, they are both located, at birth, in the same "sign" and "house" of the birth chart. And then they will seem to operate TOGETHER, along the same lines. Still, however, there is a difference between them. The Sun represents the basic conscious motive or GOAL of the personality while Saturn represents the STRUCTURAL FORM of the psyche through which the goal works outward into the world.

It is often more cataclysmic to undergo change of the "structural form" of consciousness than it is to undergo change of goal which operates THROUGH that form of consciousness.

Since we DO realize so little of what is happening in our psyches, and in their activities in our daily lives, it is perhaps well, at this point, to define what some of these parts of the personality are doing, or undergoing, particularly when the planet Saturn, by transit, is making some focus upon them, or, technically, some "aspect" to them.

In describing them, I will set an order of importance, or an order of most powerful effect, from the Saturn transits.

SATURN, at birth, of course, represents the structural form of consciousness, and its movement on from its birth place is one of the cycles to which we most powerfully respond--because it represents changes in the "projection of our individual cultural identity into the world." The transit of Saturn probably most profoundly affects the birth position of Saturn.

The SUN, in its birth position, represents the conscious PURPOSE of the life. Saturn, transitting in respect to it, is saying, "DEFINE YOUR BASIC PURPOSE or REDEFINE YOUR BASIC PURPOSE OR GOAL," and, because, the Sun also represents the source of vital energy of the psyche, it is also saying, "DISCIPLINE YOUR VITAL ENERGIES."

The MOON, in its birth position, represents the manner in which an individual APPLIES INTO DAILY ACTIVITY his basic purposes, or goals, or vitality (Sun). Saturn's transit, in respect to it, calls for a FOCUSING OF PERSONAL RESPONSES, A DISCIPLINING OF HABIT PATTERNS, A REDEFINITION OF YOUR ABILITY TO BRING YOUR PURPOSES INTO DAILY APPLICATION. It most affects habit patterns, and emotional responses that have become part of daily patterns of activity.

MERCURY, in its birth position, represents the ability to ASSIMILATE THE RESULTS OF CONTACTS WITH THE ENVIRONMENT--the thinking, communicating mechanism; the mentality. When Saturn transits in respect to Mercury, it is saying, "LEARN DEEPLY, FOCUS YOUR ABILITY TO ASSIMILATE LIFE'S CONTACTS, DEFINE YOUR PERSONAL SYSTEMS OF THINKING."

VENUS, in its birth position, represents personal and social VALUES. It also represents one's personal love life because of this-- if there's anywhere his "values" come into play, it's there. Saturn's transit, in respect to it, represents a "DEEPENING OF PERSONAL AND SOCIAL VALUES, A DEFINING OF PERSONAL LOVE RESPONSES."

MARS, in its birth position, represents personal DESIRES and the ability to ACT FORCEFULLY. It, too, often represents activities in the personal love life, but not the ones of responding to someone so much as ACTING OUT DESIRES. Saturn's transit, in respect to it, represents a "FOCUSING OF DESIRES, A DISCIPLINING OF AGGRESSIVE ACTIVITIES."

JUPITER, in its birth position, represents the ability to EXPAND YOUR PERSONAL REALM OF INFLUENCE among others. In our society, it represents "economic opportunity" and the individual's ability to be "outgoing and expansive." Saturn's transit, in respect to it, represents a "FOCUSING OF PERSONAL EXPANSIONS, A DEFINING OF APPROACHES TO OTHERS."

At this point, we have considered all the planets that represent CONSCIOUS ACTIVITY. When we move beyond them, we come to the realm of unconscious activity.

the person- ality cycles

I think we must be aware of that because only the "system's structural formative power" (TRANSITTING Saturn) can have the effect upon the individual unconscious powers that I will describe. The individual himself will not be able to do this with his own birth planets. This is one of the reasons the transits of Saturn to Uranus, Neptune and Pluto, in the individual birth chart, have never been very well described. And the latter one was not even known about before the 1930's.

Still, the system's Saturn can have a tremendous effect upon them. So I will discuss it--yet I would never admit, in delineating a birth chart, that the individual's birth Saturn (the one in his sky, rather than the sky outside) could have such an effect upon his birth Uranus, Neptune and Pluto positions.

URANUS, at birth, represents an UNCONSCIOUS INDIVIDUALITY (one over which Saturn, cultural individuality, cannot dominate)--and through that, original ideas springing up into ego-consciousness (or into Saturn's realm of control). The transit of Saturn, in respect to it, represents a "FOCUSING OF UNCONSCIOUS INDIVIDUALITY, A DEFINITION OF ORIGINAL IDEAS."

NEPTUNE, at birth, represents the ability not only to receive these ideas but to "tune in constantly to their source--a greater world of perception." Uranus brings flashes of this world, but Neptune is the umbilical cord into it. The transit of Saturn, in respect to Neptune, then, represents a "FOCUSING OF UNCONSCIOUS IMAGINATIVE POWER, A DEFINITION OF YOUR TIES WITH GREATER WORLDS OF PERCEPTION." Most people may never use this power, but they COULD. And those who do, without even consciously realizing it (which is the case, in most instances today), should realize how it is happening.

PLUTO, at birth, represents the ability not only to receive flashes from this unconscious world (Uranus) and then tie into it on a regular basis (Neptune), but to FIND A GREATER LIFE ROLE WITHIN IT. On Pluto's symbolic anvil, one forges his "role within the greater whole" whether he realizes this as a spiritual whole, a whole of humanity, or simply the whole of whatever he perceives around him that he belongs to. Saturn's transit to it, therefore, represents a "MAKING REAL OF YOUR LIFE'S GREATER ROLE, A DISCIPLINING OF YOUR COMPULSIONS." It is "compulsions" that lead most people into this role, whether it destroys their "ego" (Saturn) or gives it greater, more humanitarian, scope for activity. The former is usually the case but, again, it wouldn't HAVE to be if we would attempt to understand what is really happening in us.

Now, since most people do not really experience the transits as they could be understood, few people are going to relate to any of the interpretations except the CONJUNCTION, the first quarter SQUARE, the OPPOSITION and the last quarter SQUARE. Because of this, I will lay the greatest emphasis upon them. Actually, the majority do not experience, or live out consciously, ANY of the transits except the conjunctions when we get beyond natal Saturn and natal Sun. They seem "forced" to experience these and then they experience "relief" from them until they occur again about 30 years later. But if they would really examine their lives they would see the whole cycle operating, either unconsciously and constructively or haphazardly and disastrously.

As I say, however, we tend to ignore everything except the conjunction. So I will, of necessity, have to lay heavy stress upon it. Because the "energy flows" to all the parts of the personality are basically the same (a crescent phase sextile simply means you can now produce with that part of the personality and move constructively with it), I will not go into such detail on them. I will lay the stress upon the dynamic aspects which, in Saturn's case, cause the redefinition (conjunction), the aggressive movement forward with it (the first quarter square), the incorporation of some realization, goal or greater purpose into it (the opposition) and the final crisis toward reorientation of that part of the personality inside (the last quarter square). If one wanted to see, in great detail, what would be happening at each phase and aspect of the cycle, he could go back to the Saturn and Sun interpretations of the previous pages and simply replace the keywords used for natal Saturn and natal Sun with keywords that would be appropriate to these other parts of the conscious personality (these other natal planets).

FOCUS YOUR PERSONAL RESPONSES, DISCIPLINE YOUR HABIT PATTERNS, RE-DEFINE YOUR ABILITY TO BRING YOUR PURPOSES INTO DAILY ACTION (Saturn, by transit, is conjoining the birth Moon position. The activity begins, in a definition of the "substance" of these "habits" when Saturn enters the sign the Moon occupies. The actual habit patterns undergo powerful redefinition when Saturn conjoins the Moon by degree. The two are often indistinguishable.) For a long time now, you have been moving along on habit patterns adopted years ago. Your parents may have instilled them in you; your education may have reinforced them; your ability to survive with them may have seemed automatic up until this point. Now it is time to consider whether they are really appropriate to everything that is happening to you at this time. What could you refine--in your daily habit patterns, in your habitual emotional responses to other individuals, in your ability to bring your purposes into application-- that may NOW BE OUTMODED? If the habit patterns you have become accustomed to for years "do not work so well" anymore, it is simply time to redefine them in the light of what is REQUIRED to bring your purposes into reality. That's all that's being asked of you at this time. What is realistic, as far as changing your habitual nature is concerned, to make this possible? Now is the time to examine it. Now is the time to learn some new tricks, some new modes, some new methods, some new responses.

THE USUAL MANIFESTATION is that the individual feels "they are picking on me." Others are tearing him apart. What they are really doing is examining his habit patterns and noticing that they are no longer appropriate to what he is attempting to do, or says he is attempting to do. Sometimes he feels "my personality is being stripped bare." Things he never noticed before (and what do we notice least about ourselves, besides what has become HABITUAL?) are being pointed out as glaring parts of his inability to function in response to the demands of the immediate situation. All that's really happened is that outmoded habit patterns are becoming obvious as outmoded habit patterns--considering what MUST BE DONE. Many people feel persecuted during this period. There's something to that. Their HABITS are being persecuted, because they're no longer effective to the tasks at hand. What house has the sign Cancer on it in the birth chart? This is the field of activities in which the habits, now being redefined, will eventually have the strongest manifestation. What is happening here, now, is leading to a redefinition, later (when Saturn transits there, and with ease or difficulty according to Saturn's aspect to the birth Moon when it DOES transit there) in that realm of activity. The habits are being reformed, here and now, so that realm of activities can benefit from them later.

THE NEW PHASE is when one is quickly faced with the fact that he must adjust himself to new ways of applying his purposes into action. About 2 to 3 years after the conjunction it is possible to merge the worthwhile remnants of past habit patterns with the new ones demanded at this point, and move forward with a whole new approach to creating a functional approach to daily activities.

THE CRESCENT PHASE (about 3 to 4 years after conjunction) is a kind of "struggle forward, trying to avoid slipping into the habits of the past." There is a mobilization to do this at the semi-square aspect and that mobilization can become productive with a little effort applied at the sextile about 4 to 5 years after conjunction. Personal creativity can be applied to the new habit patters about 5 to 6 years after the conjunction.

THE FIRST QUARTER PHASE (about 7 to 8 years after conjunction) represents a time of "challenge" when the new habit patterns can be the key to functioning effectively in the face of personal crisis. One should move combatively forward with new ways to put his purposes into daily action. If he does this actively, then at 9 to 10 years after conjunction, he will find these habit patterns working creatively and easily. He has learned, through crisis, what will most effectively bring his desires into action on the daily level.

THE GIBBOUS PHASE (about 10 to 11 years after conjunction) represents a period of "perfection of personal techniques in applying your purposes into action." It's time to find out what patterns are most effective and why they have been. These you want to incorporate strongly into your activities. The ones that are superfluous you want to eliminate.

mo

NW
0-45

CR
45-90

FQ
90-135

GI
135-180

try to realize what all this perfection of personal technique is FOR. What's it going to fit into? What's its purpose? If you want to go backward, to retreat to the past, you're avoiding what's just ahead.

THE FULL PHASE (about 14 to 15 years after conjunction) represents a time when, after perfecting your personal techniques as far as responding to people in your sur-- roundings and making your habit patterns function, you begin to realize there is SOME GOAL FOR ALL THIS. You can, at this point, have a major realization about where all this instinctive activity is heading. You can, also, incorporate some larger, greater goal, INTO YOUR ABILITY TO APPLY YOUR PURPOSES INTO LIFE. Your responses and your ability to structure them are now at odds unless you DO incorporate some goal into your life and integrate your responses with a REASON for them. This is a peak of habit activity. Your habits are developed. Now what are you going to use them for that's greater than personal satisfaction that you have them? Here's where you decide. Once you do, about 1 to 2 years after the opposition, you can move away from the realization and incorporate into your personal production patterns a larger goal and a greater perfection--at the biquintile aspect that operates about 2 to 3 years after the opposition.

THE DISSEMINATING PHASE (about 3 to 4 years after opposition) represents a time WHEN YOUR INSTINCTIVE RESPONSES CAN GIVE YOU GREAT COMMUNICATIVE POWER. Your habits are now usable in what you believe, in what you want to spread. You can go about this with little trouble. You KNOW HOW to respond to people in challenging them to greater effort, to greater realizations. About 6 to 7 years after the opposition, the trine aspect operates and you have "easy ability" to make your habits, your responses and your ability to apply your purposes into conscious daily activity work creatively for you. If you have a message to convey, your very ability to use gestures will abet you in getting it across.

THE LAST QUARTER PHASE (about 8 to 9 years after opposition) represents a time when you will begin to notice, because of critical things developing inside--and they do not have to show on the surface, only you may know about them--that it's time to consider reorienting your responses to people, to situations, to life in general. If you haven't gotten a glimmer of it before, you'll get it now: some of your habit patterns are growing obsolete. They were superb for what you've already done, but they'll be outmoded for what's ahead. They will still function for you quite well on the outside, in fact, creatively in personal little ways, at the quintile which operates about 10 years after the opposition. But you should consider that you CAN CHANGE THEM IN THOUGHT, with just a little mental exercise applied, at the sextile which operates about 11 years after opposition. And if you don't, you'll soon be challenged to do so.

THE BALSAMIC PHASE (about 12 years after opposition) represents a period when you will feel, ahead of time, that THERE ARE BETTER WAYS IN WHICH YOU COULD bring your purposes into application in life. There are better things to be doing, too, especially in deciding HOW YOU'RE GOING TO RESPOND TO OTHERS IN YOUR LIFE. And now is the time to think about them. What you decide at this point, will determine the pressures upon you, at the conjunction, to change the outmoded responses and habit patterns in your life. If you decide to do so (though it will take a lot of effort), you can BEGIN making changes in these patterns about a year before the conjunction when the semi-sextile operates allowing you to merge the shards of the past (the things that will work IN ANY SITUATION) with the impetus to adjust to what's ahead.

At this point, you may think that this is a lot of words to waste on "daily habit patterns and personal responses." But if you consider just how much those things are involved in EVERYTHING YOU DO, you may change your mind about the "waste of words." Few of us realize how habitual some of our actions are--how habi- tual, even, most of our RESPONSES are. The Moon, in its positive application MEANS "the ability to be flexible, to respond to each new situation in the best manner possible." Yet we have MADE it to mean "habits that require little attention to what the situation is." That's why the conjunction of transiting Saturn with the birth Moon is such a shock to so many. They finally realize how INFLEXIBLE they have been with the one part of them that allows them to be flexible enough to adapt to any situa- tion.

(If you want to refer to the number of years involved, before conjunction or opposition, go back to the original outline of the aspects and phases involved in Saturn's transit cycle on page 61.)

ME

LEARN DEEPLY, FOCUS YOUR ABILITY TO ASSIMILATE LIFE'S CONTACTS, DEFINE YOUR PERSONAL SYSTEMS OF THINKING (Saturn is making the conjunction with natal Mercury or is entering the sign in which it's located). If you have skimmed over ideas before this time, you must now become deeply engrossed in what you are learning. It's time to organize and define your deepest reactions to the things that have been going on in your life. How HAVE you assimilated your contacts with the life around you? What is the meaning of everything, as that meaning lodges itself in your brain, your mind, your life, your systems of reaction to the world around you? This is one of the most profound learning periods you will have. Whatever sinks in now, will not be forgotten. It is time to make your thoughts deep, your communications well-considered, your personal movements well thought out. This is one of the best times of your life to be in school or in a period of learning, for what you absorb now, you will retain.

THE USUAL MANIFESTATION is a profound sense of depression. It is not so easy anymore to pass off what you say. You have to THINK before you open your mouth. For what you say sinks in with others, too. Many individuals contemplate suicide during this period for they have never come so profoundly in contact with their own thinking processes. They've never before been forced to get into the DEPTH of what's passing through their minds and their mouths. You MUST think deeply but that doesn't mean you have to sink to the bottom in despair. Is it that difficult to keep your attention on what you're learning and what your brain is letting out through your words? If it is, then something is wrong. When this period has passed, it will look much better, because whether you like it or not, you will have learned some things profoundly that you have, before this time, taken rather for granted. This is not a time for creative or sporadic thinking or communicating; it's a time for PROFOUND thinking and sensible communicating. It is an excellent time to grasp the depth, the technical meaning, or the seriousness of anything.

THE NEW PHASE is a time when you spontaneously realize that you must come to terms with life on a thoughtful basis. Old thoughts will not suffice. Old means of communicating will not, either. Your brain is undergoing a work session. Let it. Let it probe deeply. What is it you really want to LEARN from life? You're headed toward it, now, without even knowing it. What you already HAVE learned can be merged with this new knowledge at the semi-sextile, but not without effort.

THE CRESCENT PHASE is the period when you "struggle forward" to find out from life what it is you have come to learn. You mobilize your thinking powers and you let them lead you out of past patterns of thought. At the sextile, it will take only a little effort for this to result in productive thinking and productive communicating. At the quintile shortly after, you can be personally creative in moving away from past thought patterns and incorporating new "systems" into your own ability to operate in your surroundings.

THE FIRST QUARTER PHASE presents you with some kind of crisis in your ability to communicate and your ability to organize your thoughts. Your mind will be challenged by happenings in your surroundings. It will be challenged to go forth on new thought patterns of adaptability and personal flexibility. If you survive this crisis of the mentality, it will be easy for you to adopt a new creative line of communicating. Your brain has now got to RELATE TO YOUR SURROUNDINGS because you're being personally challenged to do so. Out of this crisis will come one of the great creative periods of your life in analyzing, communicating, setting up systems of thought that allow you to operate as a real individual even if you don't yet realize what this is all leading toward.

THE GIBBOUS PHASE challenges you to spend a period of apprenticeship in learning how to APPLY your thinking to the personal problems of your life. There are many questions you have to ask and many problems your thinking will have to solve. Your ability to communicate can be somewhat acid, irritating others into sometimes edgy

NW
0-45

CR
45-90

FQ
90-135

GI
135-180

the personality cycles

**FU
180-135**

**DI
135-90**

**LQ
90-45**

**BA
45-0**

responses to your talk and your questioning. Ignore this. Move on aggressively, but at the same time with the CAPACITY TO LEARN FROM EXPERIENCE. Adopt some of the techniques you see working for others. Analyze your systems of thinking and operating on your thoughts. Exclude from your personal "systems" what is cumbrous or superfluous. Hone down your ability to put words to use. This will become a productive technique you will have learned thoroughly at the biquintile. You can establish a kind of "personal trademark" in your communicating, in your writing, in your ability to set up systems for daily operation. At the quincunx there will be a tendency to get so involved in these "details of productive communicating" that you will forget what they are FOR. Don't fall too deeply into this. It's an irritation that is keeping your mind alive. Life doesn't want you to become an "automaton;" it simply wants you to get your thinking in shape and your systems for communicating in working order.

THE FULL PHASE is a time of personal revelation, realization. You can now incorporate some GOAL into your ability to operate productively on the mental plane. You will be challenged now to THINK CAREFULLY before you speak, before you communicate, before you operate within your personal "systems." What is all your talking FOR? WHY do you have the capacity to think? What good is it doing you or anybody else? Many people come along to this point and find there are "obstacles" to their thoughts, to their talk, to their ability to get their ideas across. There is only one reason for this: it is possible their thought has no value to anyone but themselves. This should not be so. If the world is going to listen to you, you have got to have something of value to offer it through yourself. This is the period when you can get it. As soon as you do, when the illumination comes, you can move away from the experience with the quincunx and go forward to communicate with this new CONTENT added to your power to communicate, to learn, to set up systems of operation. And this will extend to a new TECHNICAL ABILITY at the biquintile.

THE DISSEMINATING PHASE is the great period of getting your ideas across, of popularizing them, of circulating them through your very deeds and actions. You can come across vividly to people now because you have learned from life and you have something to say that you believe in, that you know by personal conviction. This can be a crowning period in any activity that requires you to get your ideas across to other people. You have learned for this very purpose. Now, you can live out what you have learned. The challenge is there when the phase begins--the challenge to go forth with your personal message, whether this is a simple "living out of what you believe in what you are doing" or whether it's the ability to sway people to your ideas or ideas that you've learned from others that you feel are worthy. Once you have accepted this challenge, the trine aspect begins to operate and it is easy to get those ideas moving, to get yourself moving into what you are doing. You are personally creative now and you are conscious of it. This is the apex of the thinking process in your life.

THE LAST QUARTER PHASE brings a challenge from inside to begin reorienting your thinking. You can actually be trying to suppress some very radical thoughts that are coming up from inside. This can bring you a "crisis inside." You don't have to reveal it; you don't even have to act upon it at all so that others, outside you, can see that you are doing so. But you DO HAVE TO ACCEPT THE INNER CHALLENGE for what it is-- a glimmer of what is to come later in your life when this thinking, learning cycle begins again on another level. At the sextile aspect you can productively go about accepting this inside; you can even go inside and prepare a mental "image" change for yourself. The quintile which preceded it will have given you the personal creativity of mind to do so if you will accept it.

THE BALSAMIC PHASE is a time of mobilization of your thoughts into some new major line or orientation. You may ignore this if you want, but if you do, then you are LIKELY to be depressed under the next transitting Saturn conjunction to birth Mercury's position. What have you learned, what have you communicated, what personal systems have worked for you over the past 30 years? Well, they've gotten you this far, but now they're outmoded. It's time for a change of mind--one that will lead you toward the future. It's time for a major new period of learning through life and communicating what you have learned--no matter how small, or how modest, that may be in your life.

VE

The whole previous 30-year thinking, learning, communicating process, as described, is related to the ACTIVITIES of the houses in your birth chart that bear the signs (on their cusps) Gemini and Virgo. What you learn through this Saturn cycle can be APPLIED in those fields of activity in your life. What you learn is most likely to COME INTO MANIFESTATION in those activities. Consider that. The Gemini house will involve you in what you learn most personally. The Virgo house's activities will manifest what you have learned as "an adjustment to the world outside yourself."

DEEPEN YOUR VALUES, DISCIPLINE YOUR PERSONAL NEEDS, DEFINE YOUR SOCIAL RESPONSES (Saturn has entered the sign in which your birth Venus is located). It's time to go into yourself and decide what you really DO value in life. Do you have it or are you still looking for it? What is it that you most want to RECEIVE from others? You're likely to learn very profoundly now about that. You are also likely to have to define your social responses to others, or redefine them, because they are becoming obsolete to what is ahead of you. It's time to think deeply about what you value in this life, because if you don't feel it's there, you are about to go looking for it-- once you decide, profoundly, what it is. This applies, too, to your social life and what you seek in it.

THE USUAL MANIFESTATION is that the individual suddenly feels "I am unloved." Those he cares about do not show him much attention. Maybe the reason is that they are not what he really wants in his life. Maybe the actual reason is that he is isolated in himself, now, trying to determine what he DOES value and whether the people and things around him actually fit the specifications he has unconsciously set, or had set for him, and is now coming to realize consciously. On the personal level, this is a time when many marriages break up because the person experiencing the transit feels his partner is not truly demonstrating affection. Well, it actually works both ways. The individual himself is not receiving affection very well. He is also pondering whether or not that person in his life is what he actually wanted--whether he ever thought about this before or not. It is certainly not a time of joy in one's social life. He begins to see people for what they have actually been to him, and for him. He begins to see profoundly how lacking some of this has been for what he really values. If a person is materially oriented, many things he has acquired now need fixing up to MAINTAIN, or increase, their value on the material level.

THE NEW PHASE is a time when one plunges profoundly into a state where he realizes he must define for himself what he does value and then check to see if it exists in his life. Many adopt NEW VALUES at this time because the old ways they were taught to love, or to value another, or even things, are no longer adequate. This is quite a deep realization in many lives. But one should push ahead with it. He should stumble on, if necessary, to come nearer to what he truly feels he values when this transit is in effect. At the semi-sextile he can realize what PARTS of what he has so far loved or valued, are valid to what he's beginning to realize is necessary for him to have.

NW
0-45

THE CRESCENT PHASE represents a time when one "struggles away from the old and becomes a new person in search of new values." This is often the time when an individual, who has broken up a love affair or a marriage, finds himself struggling forward with the realization that he must find something to replace that which was inadequate or only superficial. At the sextile, this struggle can turn productive. One can begin finding, in others, what he was seeking as a result of the conjunction's effect upon him.

CR
45-90

THE FIRST QUARTER PHASE can bring him a challenge, or a crisis, in his love life or in his search for personal values. Some people feel they are getting nowhere in their search because the obstacles around them are overwhelming. They must accept this challenge, though, because soon after it appears there can be an easy flow of understanding and acceptance. The crisis, in love or in the search, can turn into a creative resolution of their problems when the trine aspect operates. But the crisis PRODUCES it.

FQ
90-135

THE GIBBOUS PHASE is a time when one analyzes what he has come to value since the conjunction, when he learns personal techniques for making it operate effectively

GI
135-180

the person- ality cycles

FU 180-135

DI 135-90

LQ 90-45

BA 45-0

and practically. At the biquintile, his personal technique of handling ideas or people becomes an asset to making values operate strongly for him. At the quincunx he has an irritating habit of wondering whether all he has done is really true or worthwhile. But he must move through this because a major realization is about to set in.

THE FULL PHASE is a time when the world around you, or the circumstances in effect, will make an individual realize that "you must think before you act--particularly toward anything or anyone you value or you will find it eluding you." This is often a crisis, again, in a person's love life because he does not really KNOW what he wants--he only pursues what he's become accustomed to pursuing and there's a major illumination he must now face about that. If he's done what's true to him, instinctively, he now needs to do it because he REALIZES what he values. Because he KNOWS. Because it has CONTENT AND MEANING in his life. During this period, too, he must integrate his personal needs with the world's demands or his loves and his searches for value will fall apart on him because they will encounter outside "obstacles." The question is this: Does what you value help you in being aware of others, or does it impair that awareness in you? If the first is true, this will be a tremendous period of realization for you. If the second is true, this can be a personally shattering time in your life.

THE DISSEMINATING PHASE is a period of your life when what you value, or who you value, can suffuse everything you do. A person you love for a good reason--because it adds to you and helps you add to others--can make you certain of yourself, able to communicate the love you feel for them to others and to everything you're doing in life. BECAUSE YOU ARE IN LOVE, with life or another person, you become vivid in your ability to relate what you believe, what you have learned, what you VALUE. For anyone who has found what he does value, in a life's effort or in another person, this can be a highly romantic and creative period, particularly when the trine aspect operates, making things easily productive, after the sesquiquadrate's challenge to take what you value out into the world and convey it to others.

THE LAST QUARTER PHASE is a time to re-orient, or rethink, consciously your values and your personal loves. You are going through some kind of change inside. You are either becoming a different kind of person or you are going through a required change in some major department of life. It's bound to affect the others in your life and it's bound to affect what you manifest from here on. Can you make this creative? Can you relate to what you are doing, or who you care for, in a different way for different reasons? Can you be flexible in your life of personal and social values? Well, you'll be thinking about this even if you don't talk about it. And it will be leading you to an inner conversion. Which you can handle with just a little effort when the sextile operates. At that time, you can go through inner changes which will make you more capable of being FLEXIBLE with what you value.

THE BALSAMIC PHASE is a time of mutation in your values. Is what you want, is what you care for, oriented at all to what there is left, now, of your life? You're going to become a different person, soon. You're going to VALUE things for different reasons than you have before. What you have done so far and loved so far has brought you to this point in life. If you can change, and it can change, you'll have no troubles ahead. If you, or it, is inflexible, you're going to feel "lonely," "unloved" and in trouble when the Saturn conjunction of your birth Venus, by transit, arrives again in a few years. Here's where you make the DECISION CONSCIOUSLY that you can change your values to fit what your life is aimed toward. If you don't make that decision, you will be forced into it by circumstances at the conjunction.

What house in your birth chart has the sign Taurus on it? Here is where the values you change are going to manifest most strongly in personal things. What house has the sign Libra on its cusp? This is the field of activities in which your redefined, more profound, sense of values is going to color your life socially and in the eyes of others.

In other words, the changes in your PERSONAL VALUES are going to manifest into the realm where Taurus operates in you. The changes in your SOCIAL VALUES are going to manifest most strongly in the activities which are colored, at your birth, by the sign Libra.

FOCUS YOUR DESIRES: DISCIPLINE YOUR AGGRESSIONS (Saturn is transitting the sign in which Mars is located at birth; the attitude to desires and aggressions comes under discipline when it enters the sign; the actual desires and aggressions come under control when it meets Mars by degree). This is a time when an individual needs to consider carefully his actions and his aggressive tendencies. Where have they led him so far and what do they actually have to do with what is going on in his life now? This is a period when over-aggressiveness can be met with resistance from the outside. All that is happening is a need to focus one's desires so he knows what actions and situations they are creating in his life. It is also a time when it is appropriate to discipline one's physical energies. What is it that you really do desire and where does this fit into your life pattern? How are your physical energies actually contributing to what you're doing? It's time to review all that and redefine your actual desire nature. It may have been propelling you along a course that was not at all appropriate to the other major lines of endeavor in your life now. It's time to find out. It's also time to discipline your energies to the actual production of what's most important at this time in your life.

THE USUAL MANIFESTATION is that the individual feels his "desires are being thwarted," his tendencies to act first, and think later, are being met with heavy resistance from outside forces. Any over-aggressiveness he displays is likely to be met by obstacles in the environment. This can extend so far as to be disciplined by people in authority because his personal actions are "too rash." Many individuals come up against the police and other authorities (represented by Saturn, the form of discipline in the world) at this time. And there is only one reason. Their actions are not well thought out. They are pushing too hard along a line they have not really thought out. Some individuals actually experience physical setbacks because they have IGNORED the fact that their energies should be disciplined to the tasks that are important. The point of the whole transit is that one should learn WHERE his personal desires are leading him. If they are not defined, or directed, to the overall goals that allow his potential to operate then he will probably meet all kinds of resistance until they are. It is important, at this time, to DIRECT one's personal desires and his physical energies, because they will operate spontaneously for some time once they are aligned to the mental or spiritual goal to which he fuses them at this conjunction.

THE NEW PHASE is a time, after the person has directed his energies and desires toward his goals, that he can move spontaneously on the physical and emotional level. He should plunge in, with passion, moving on the ideas and activities that are pushing his goals toward fruition. He has a kind of charisma, or magnetism, because of the WAY he moves toward his goals--once his desires and physical energies are geared toward them.

THE CRESCENT PHASE is a time when one must watch that past desires, and past habits of aggressiveness, do not creep back into his activities. It is almost as if he is meeting the resistance of his surroundings in moving forward. His desires must be geared to the future, his energies working along lines that will propel him there. At the sextile aspect it is easy, with just a little effort put into it, to PUSH forward toward those goals. In the quintile aspect period, it is possible to put personal style and personal creativity into one's movements and activities.

THE FIRST QUARTER PHASE can bring a physical or emotional crisis to challenge the individual--to ask him, through action, "Are your desires wedded to your goals, are your actions contributing to your basic purpose?" An individual can be extremely combative at this time, but he will also feel that there are obstacles in the surroundings that are meeting his activity with resistance. If his goal is focused, even unconsciously, these obstacles are there to challenge him toward a more creative APPLICATION of energy, to fuse his desires so strongly with his goals that he can tear down all that resists what he is becoming that is new and self-expressive. If the goal is NOT focused, this can be a time of extreme opposition to desires and energies and it will be easy to run into opposition head-on. Let yourself move forward, if your goal is focused, and this physical, emotional challenge will lead to the creation of a new overall attitude at the trine aspect, when action will become easy and flow forward with little effort.

the person- ality cycles

MA

the person- ality cycles

THE GIBBOUS PHASE is a time to employ actual techniques of using physical energy in the tasks at hand. If you have to spend a period of apprenticeship learning how to channel your animal energies into your goals, this is where it will happen. Examine how your energy fits your goals. Try to decide how you could use it better. At the biquintile it is easy to develop patterns of action that will continue to make you productive in your activities.

THE FULL PHASE is a time when you must KNOW, consciously, HOW your energies and your desires are abetting your goals and your activities. If they are in the way of what you are doing--if your personal aggressiveness, your animal desires and your physical actions--are not contributing to your goals BECAUSE YOU HAVE MADE THEM DO SO, then, again, aggressions meet resistance. Personal desires are once more thwarted and one's energies seem to be thwarted. This is another time when, if energy is not geared to conscious goals, there can be trouble with people in authority and the individual can feel he is being thwarted by outside forces beyond his control.

THE DISSEMINATING PHASE is when the animal energy in an individual's makeup can give him a magnetism in putting forth what he believes, in building to a climax a line of activity. It is desire that moves most of us to action. Desire now can be channeled into what one believes, making it vivid because even his actions are saying that this is real, it is worthwhile, it is put forth because experience has convinced him it should be.

THE LAST QUARTER PHASE brings a crisis in the mind that asks this simple question: Are the desires that move you really fitted to what you can see ahead? Are your energies geared to a new cycle of activity that you can feel coming? If not, you should begin amending them in your mind and finding ways to re-align them to some major goal that will manifest in the next seven years. This is not combat from outside, but combat from inside, asking you to align, practically, your desires and energies with your activities.

THE BALSAMIC PHASE is when you reformulate your desire nature so that it propels you toward whatever activity is next in line for manifestation. You will get a good glimpse here, of how some of your desires could be rechanneled into activities that no longer fit what you have been engaged in before. Your loves and personal pursuits could come in for some startling conversions at this period because you will soon be plunged into another round of physical action. And now is the time to decide, consciously, what that will be geared toward--even if it completely contradicts everything you've desired before.

FOCUS YOUR EXPANSIONS, DEFINE YOUR APPROACHES TO OTHERS (Saturn is entering the sign in which Jupiter was located at birth--the attitudes involved in your ability to expand your realm of influence undergo definition when it enters the sign; the actual projects involved can emerge when it reaches Jupiter's birth degree). This is a time of your life when you must examine how you are building your place in society in practical terms. How do you go about facing the practical realities of the world in which you live. Now is the time to consider some SOLID foundations for your operations in society. The flashy little things that get you here and there for moments are not the things that this transit calls for examining. It calls you to examine the practical foundations you will use in society over a LONG PERIOD OF TIME. How could you build them better? How could you be methodical in expanding them? How could you build them firmly so there will be something you can ALWAYS rely on in times ahead?

THE USUAL MANIFESTATION is some kind of opportunity that comes to you in the form of a minor advance that will have to be worked on for some time to make it outstanding. Yet the basis of something extremely lasting and firm in its makeup is there if you can perceive it. What happens to most people is that in a period when they're looking for some major opportunity, a smaller one emerges. If it isn't beneath them to take something and build it thoroughly from the ground up, this proves, later, to be one of the most solid opportunities life ever offered them. They start it here and it reaches climax at the opposition. In other words, it can take 15 years to build this thing if it's an economic opportunity. If its a WAY of approaching people so that, in general, you can function practically in society, it may not take so long to build it, but it will still reach its greatest ability to function 15 years later.

THE NEW PHASE is a time to plunge into practical activity that will SLOWLY expand
your realm of influence among other people. Do this instinctively, but consider that
you are BUILDING WITH PATIENCE for the future. Plunge into some small thing and
make it grow. Your ability to be PRACTICAL in expanding your realm of influence is
a key force that can now be acted upon spontaneously.

THE CRESCENT PHASE is a time of struggle to make this thing, which didn't seem too
impressive to begin with, slowly take shape--even if everything in the surroundings
seems to smirk at you while you are doing it. Don't listen to the voices of the past--
move on toward the future. You know you can make this something firm in foundation;
that's what you're doing now, as a matter of fact--laying the foundations for your own
economic or social future. The struggle will turn into a productive movement forward
at the sextile if you aren't overwhelmed by the doubts of surrounding people and forces.

THE FIRST QUARTER PHASE is a time to face the challenge of obstacles in what you
are building. You have moved forward--now some crisis can come that seems to
threaten what is already a movement that requires patience. Face that challenge. Act
and persevere. This challenge comes because you can turn it into a creative building
force at the trine when the situation will ease off and you will again move slowly on.

THE GIBBOUS PHASE is a time to analyze the techniques you are using in building whatever project you have been engaged in for about 8 years. Spend some time learning
any methods of operation that will help you continue building. Sort out the superfluous
from the necessary and you will find that your own techniques for operating become much
more productive at the biquintile.

THE FULL PHASE is a time when whatever it was you started at the conjunction should
be completed in FORM. Is this a "way of operating?" Is it an actual project? Which-
ever, it is now time to add some content to it. It's time to look at what you've been doing from the outside. What's the future goal of this operation or project? At this point
you MUST KNOW WHAT YOU ARE DOING AND WHY or it will seem worthless. It took
a long time to build, anyway; now it must hold some meaning in others' eyes, too.

THE DISSEMINATING PHASE is the period when this project or method of operating to
make your way through society finally proves its worth. It will be obvious, now, once
you precipitate what you are doing, consciously into the surroundings, that you believe
this project of your, or this way of operating of yours, is worthwhile. If it's a matter
of need of recognition for you or it, this is the time when it can happen most effectively.
This is when a business, a project, a way of surviving, can operate most effectively.

THE LAST QUARTER PHASE is a time to consider some new way of making your way
in society. A voice inside will be trying to tell you that you have used this situation about
as far as it will go. Now, it's time to think of something else and start getting ready to
move out of this one particular situation you have been operating with for 21 years.

THE BALSAMIC PHASE is the period when you can actually picture in your mind the
kind of slow-building, but firmly founded, activity you next want to engage in. It's also
a time when you can find a much more effective way--one that's geared to the future--
rather than the past, to operate in social terms. Nothing lasts forever. Decide, here,
what you'd really like to do that will take you some time to build--that will be practical
but worthwhile--and you can easily meet it in reality at the next conjunction. This is the
time of thinking, and imaging, before the project, or way of operating, actually emerges.

FOCUS YOUR INDIVIDUALITY: DEFINE YOUR ORIGINAL IDEAS (Saturn is transitting
the sign in which your birth Uranus is located. The ideas are there when it enters the
sign; they can manifest in forms when it enters the birth degree). This can be one of
the most original periods of your life in PUTTING INTO ACTUAL FORM WHAT YOU
HAVE ALWAYS THOUGHT WOULD MAKE YOU MOST INDIVIDUAL. It's time to take
all those ideas that have been flashing through your head, on and off, for years--rather
haunting you in the midst of the necessity of just surviving--and put them into some
tangible form that will leave an impression on the world. It's also time to put REALITY
into what your concept of "being individual" means.

the person-ality cycles

UR

nw
0-45

CR
45-90

FQ
90-135

GI
135-180

FU
180-135

DI
135-90

Put yourself into forms that people can see. If you're a writer, you will be amazed, when this period is over, how TANGIBLY your creative powers worked. If you're an inventor, or individualist, this is the time when your genius comes into actual working dimensions. You must sit down and let this happen, or spend some time at MAKING it happen, but it is the one transit in the sky in which REALITY actually aids and abets the impulse to REBELLION and originality.

THE USUAL MANIFESTATION is exactly what is said, if the individual is one who has any center of awareness. It is easy, if one sits still long enough to let it happen, to become original in actual activity. If one will not, then another thing happens. He makes some ridiculous, grand rebellion against life that is extremely unconsidered and he meets tremendous resistance. This is because he is not APPLYING INDIVIDUALITY INTO LIFE but is simply being rebellious for rebellion's sake. This is another transit that can bring one into conflict with authority--particularly if he things "I can get away with anything." If what one is doing has some actual application that is beyond himself, there's likely to be little trouble. If it's merely an action to bolster an otherwise weak-ened ego, he's likely to be in a lot. This is a time when one can PATIENTLY bring into application his own particular genius, individuality or originality OR it's a time when his senseless, ego-propping rebellions bring him into conflict with established authority. It usually has a lot to do with his own personal patience. If he is patient enough to SPEND TIME bringing individuality into an actual application in the world, he will hardly be in trouble. If he wants everything this minute, he dooms himself.

THE NEW PHASE is a time to plunge instinctively and spontaneously into the activity that has been haunting one's mind for a long time. That doesn't mean to plunge into it for one moment, but to plunge in, with commitment, for this plunge will last for several years and it is almost as if an inner genius is taking over one's actions.

THE CRESCENT PHASE is a struggle forward out of a past that has been overly pattern-ed and overly-conventional. The new ideas that are now pouring out of one are a challenge to that old view of oneself. They are lifting him toward an undefined future but the "feeling" of it is so strong, that he is becoming a representative of what it means whether he's personally aware of it or not. This is no time to go back to the old familiar patterns; follow that inner genius--it's moving to a far better place to be.

THE FIRST QUARTER PHASE is a time when the individual is challenged to step up this production of original ideas that began at the conjunction. Those things are turned out, or should have been. They can't just lie there. They must move out into the world--through the individual himself. That is the challenge. To take these ideas and move out with them. The challenge is now to meet the resistance to anything new, to learn how to move through that resistance, and then the forward motion is easy.

THE GIBBOUS PHASE is a time when the individual can learn some techniques for bringing his ideas more effectively into action. He should get rid of old habits. He should spend time learning anything that will allow him to be an individual more strongly. He may come across some new idea, or some new person, who can help him in this.

THE FULL PHASE is when the whole operation that began at the conjunction can reach a climax. Now, it is not so important to be inventive and original as it is to have some GREATER GOAL for what has been passing through oneself. The surroundings will challenge the individual so that he will consider HOW his ideas can be applied more effectively into others' lives. If he is simply a rebellious crank, he will meet resistance once more. If he is not, all he does is gear his individuality more to the surroundings and the needs of others. If he refused to be an individual back at the conjunction--actually if he refused to allow ideas to move through him--his life can fall apart here just because he did. It can seem empty of any meaning that makes him more than a cog in society's wheels.

THE DISSEMINATING PHASE is the time when the individual's ideas can get the greatest reception from the surroundings, partly because they were geared to have meaning for others, partly because of the conviction he puts into them. This can be the crowning period of an 18-year period of putting individual ideas into tangible forms and activities.

It all depends on what the individual did back at the conjunction. If he functioned spontaneously, then, letting ideas move outward through him from the unconscious force of
individuality within him (in other words if he sat his Saturn down so his Uranus could
work outward through it), he is not likely to be able to desert this originality and
the disseminating period is simply a climax manifestation of it--but one that comes
consciously, rather than spontaneously. If he fell back, or fell apart at other steps
along the way from the conjunction, it is possible he can regain some of that ability to
allow individuality to flow through his cultural ego at the disseminating phase. There
is a great call to that for everyone--even if the originality comes through some other
person and is only spoken through the individual we are seeing because he wants something greater than himself to believe in.

THE LAST QUARTER PHASE is a challenge from inside to consider some newer, more
demanding ideas to set the person on an even greater course of unfolding individuality.
Some people feel as if they are getting radical ideas, inside themselves--as if some
hidden geni were whispering dangerous words into their ears. And they are not far
wrong. Whatever is rumbling inside now IS dangerous to the cultural identity that has
been established through the Saturn cycle of transit to its own position--particularly if
that cycle has created nothing new than what was there at about age 30. The voice of
discontent operates from inside, again, calling the individual to move, at least intellectually, toward ideas that can be lived out through him at the next conjunction.

THE BALSAMIC PHASE is where those ideas really haunt the person. They will be
sitting right there in front of his mind, saying, "You COULD be me." Or, "You
COULD be this." All the individual has to do is become very much involved in them
and make a conscious commitment to live them out and he has forged his partnership
with a greater destiny than his culture, probably, has taught him is possible. It is
here that the ideas wing through his mind and call him to the meeting with a new idea
of his inner self that is coming at the conjunction. If he can accept the challenge, and
do it consciously now, knowing that what he has done so far is of the past, and what
he means to do from here on is of the future, all he will have to do IS sit his Saturn
ego down when the conjunction comes and let the Uranus forces in him operate outward
into the world THROUGH that Saturn form.

        From this point on, I will not describe the phases of the Saturn cycle of
transit, except to mark some especially critical points. Most of us do not know how to
use the Neptune and Pluto forces in us. Most of us do not even want to ALLOW THEM
to operate THROUGH us. The intelligent person WANTING to unfold his own potential,
even the spiritual or unconscious potential, MAY want to do so. If he does, then it is
partly his use of his own intelligence that will make it possible. In that case, it will be
easy for him to see, by now, what each of these "phases" is saying essentially. All
he will have to understand is what Neptune and Pluto represent and let them unfold as
they move along through the eight phases--or, realistically, as they move along into
activation because of Saturn's movement to them.

        I will also describe the transit of Saturn over the Part of Fortune and Nodes
but will not consider it so much a cycle, though it could be one if we allowed ourselves
to perceive the various agencies of personality and unconscious awareness operating
in us. They all DO operate on cycles, even if we only FEEL TUMULTUOUSLY the
conjunctions that bring those cycles into operation.

FOCUS YOUR IMAGINATION. DEFINE YOUR TIES WITH GREATER WORLDS OF
PERCEPTION (Saturn is transitting the sign in which Neptune was located at your
birth). In a slightly different way than with Uranus, this can be one of the most imaginative periods of your life. It is time to take the ideas, with which you make CONSTANT
contact, and bring them into some tangible form. If you are musical, intuitive, artistic
or creative in any sustained way, this is your great working period of producing some
of the forms you have made contact with in more than ordinary ways. This is often a
time of production for the creative individual--a time when it seems it is easy to put
into FORM what he has been DREAMING about for some time. If an individual has ever
felt that there are parts of him, beyond the mind, with which he is in contact, this
is a period when he can establish CONCRETE WAYS of bringing those parts down into

**the
person-
ality
cycles**

**LQ
90-45**

**BA
45-0**

NE

the person-ality cycles

what he is doing in this world. For anyone who works in a glamor industry, this is a time when he makes illusions tangible forces in his life. There is nothing wrong with illusions, so long as we realize what they are in the light of the kind of perceptions we have operating in our sensory, dimensional world. If one can understand that, this can be an extremely beautiful period of his life. If he cannot, it can be a period when he sinks deeply into illusions and feels he has been deceived by them. He hasn't; but his sensory perceptions have if they believe what they have envisioned is real.

THE USUAL MANIFESTATION is that the individual, proceeding for some time on a pattern of deceptions in his life, or in regard to other individuals in his life, comes face to face with the reality of just how far those deceptions have invaded his realm of operation. If the individual is DECEIVING anyone, himself, this is likely to be brought out into the open. Sometimes, because one calls upon the powers of the "unconscious" to get through life, and then attempts to believe these are parts of his own ego at work, he has some of his "cherished illusions" shattered in rather unexpected and even seemingly "strange" ways. People who have used the power of "glamour" and "illusion" in projecting themselves either have to find more definitive ways of doing so or they discover that old ways of doing this are becoming outmoded. Some people have what they call "shattering psychic experiences." And, often, this happens because they tend to equate what they are calling "psychic" with material values. People who use drugs, or alcohol, to an excess, can find this a very depressing and difficult period. It's the perfect time for a "bad trip" if one is overdoing drugs and the logical time for "conflict with authority" if one is into alcohol too deeply. Whatever happens, it seems "strange" and often "unexplainable" to the logical mind of the individual. And this is simply because he refuses to recognize the actual reality of the "intuitive" state of existence. The house in the birth chart that bears the sign Pisces is where later effects of whatever happens here can materialize in a different form.

IF ONE WOULD USE THIS TRANSIT, the New phase is a logical time to plunge into the process of making dreams come real or putting imagination into tangible forms; the First Quarter phase would be a period when one would move these forms out into his surroundings and face some kind of challenge that could result in a creative resolution. The opposition would be a period when he would have to gear these forms of the imagination to the circumstances of the world around him in order that, in the Disseminating phase, he could live out their validity or communicate them strongly. The Last Quarter phase would represent a call from inside to bring his structured awareness into this world of imagination and let it dissolve somewhat into a new form of perception that could be lived out spontaneously at the next conjunction.

MAKE REAL YOUR LIFE 'ROLE;' DISCIPLINE YOUR COMPULSIONS (Saturn is transitting the sign in which Pluto is located at birth). It is time to plunge into it, even if you do not truly understand it consciously, the greater role into which your life can be shaped. If you can do it, it is time to face, in real terms, an "initiation into a greater form of life activity." This can be because you feel compelled to go beyond the cramping forms of "social identity" or it can be because you want a real transformation of yourself to occur inside. Have you ever felt that you could be "reborn" as an individual and begin to realize that life has more meaning than what people around you take for granted. If you have not, your life could be plunged into a crisis, now, involving matters of the house where Pluto is located at your birth. You will probably be compelled to undergo a slow transformation of your perception of these things, at the least; at the most, you may undergo some slow crisis, that comes to a head as Pluto's birth degree is reached by transitting Saturn. Whatever happens, it can entirely reform your life--in the matters of the activities where Pluto is operating at your birth. If you believe "death" is a matter of "transformation," rather than an end, you will be well prepared for this period. There is no necessity for an individual to die--but some part of his awareness as it was originally operating in these matters will die and something greater (probably because of the experience encountered now) will take its place.

THE USUAL MANIFESTATION is a feeling of compulsion to plunge into some activity that the individual would never have considered before this time. What he doesn't realize is that something inside is compelling him so he will get a larger perception of what he could be. Many lives are struck by tumultuous events at this time. They're unaware of what happened. Pluto's realm of activity is not one of conscious realization. It is one of unconscious initiation into greater, more encompassing, more community-conscious activity. This may be brought about through "forceful events" or it may be brought about quite simply by the individual being receptive to something greater occurring in those matters of his life. Some individuals experience life-shattering events; others do not. There is no way of telling what will happen. Occurrences are geared only to one thing: this life must be shaped, in real ways, into activities (in this house) that are of benefit to everyone as well as to the individual himself. It is the most selfish, ego-centered individuals who seem to reel under the blow of Pluto's being transitted by Saturn. Those who can see the value of doing for others, as well as themselves, often do not even experience it.

IF ONE USED THIS CYCLE, he would plunge, instinctively, into activities that would transform his life at the New phase. He would struggle forward from the confining routines of previous activities at the Crescent phase and at the First Quarter phase he would face the challenge of moving his transformed activities out into the surroundings in ways that help others as well as himself. His creative crisis would involve things like that. At the Gibbous phase he would find the techniques that would perfect his ability to operate as one who is helping others as well as himself--as one who is integrated into a greater whole than himself. At the opposition he would again be challenged-- this time to allow larger concepts of operation to come into play in this transformed "role" of his in society. At the Disseminating phase he would be living out that role consciously and creatively and at the Last Quarter phase he would accept the challenge from inside to consider how this role could be made even more effective. At the Balsamic phase he would be prepared to be initiated into an even greater manifestation of making his life of worth to everyone and at the next conjunction he would once more plunge into an initiation into a larger role that would lead him into more activities.

MAKE REAL YOUR GAINS; DEFINE YOUR POWERS OF SELF-INTEGRATION (Saturn is transitting the North Node of the Moon). This is a time when you must realistically face the question: "Are you an integrated person. Do your ego-goals and your unconscious powers operate together?" If you can answer this affirmatively, you are likely simply to find a very realistic, and effective, way of pursuing directions that MAKE you an integrated personality. If you can't, you are likely to feel "frustrated" in being able to pursue what you consider your greatest direction of growth. If this is so, you should consider again what IS your direction for growth and integration. Are you sure you are not following the path of least resistance. If you have never REALIZED CONSCIOUSLY how to integrate yourself as an individual you are likely to come across some very practical ways of doing so. You will have to be patient in making them operate

CURB YOUR TENDENCY TO ESCAPE: DEFINE YOUR ACCUMULATED ASSETS AND HOW YOU ARE USING THEM (Saturn is transitting the South Node of the Moon). If you are running merrily through life on the path of least resistance you are likely to come to an abrupt halt at this time. And it may be because the things you took for granted are now drying up on you. You suddenly overdrew your account of accumulated assets. You may also meet people who interfere "fatefully" with your life and become a "drag" on your ability to coast along. What you should understand is that the South Node of the Moon, by house position at your birth, shows where you have accumulated assets that can be called upon in an EMERGENCY or that can be RELEASED to other people. You should not be indulging in them, yourself, in order to escape the challenges your birth pattern poses at the North Node. If you don't release these assets yourself, at the time Saturn crosses over the node (or if you have made ill use of them), something like "fate" is likely to do it for you.

DEFINE YOUR SELF-EXPRESSION: MAKE REAL AND PROFOUND YOUR SEARCH FOR HAPPINESS (Saturn is transitting the Part of Fortune). It's time to decide what is the most "effective" way of expressing yourself in order that you can find personal happiness. If your casual way of self-expression is a burden on others, you are likely to find a lot out about that now. If it isn't; then you will merely find more effective ways of allowing it to operate. What you must realize now is that your ability to express yourself must be a REAL AND ACTUAL contribution to finding personal happiness.

the person- ality cycles

RELAX A LITTLE: TAKE THIS TIME TO REVIEW YOUR SITUATION AND WHAT YOU HAVE BEEN ABLE TO DO WITH IT (Saturn, by transit, is retrograde in motion-- it is backing off from the conjunction, square or oppsotion of one of your birth planets, or it is retrograding into the sign it occupied before it entered this one). Whatever responsibilities you've been forced to assume, whatever realities you've had to face, it's time now to relax a little and look over what you've done. Have you actually faced the situation that needed definition? What have you done about it? Could you handle it better in some way? Now's the time to think about that because the retrograde movement of Saturn is GIVING YOU TIME TO REVIEW YOUR SITUATION. This is not a complete respite because direct motion will resume sometime in the near future. Meanwhile, this period is best used to see what methods, what techniques, what applications of effort could be better employed to face the situation that is undergoing definition. Do you see now what has been happening? The intelligence of the "system" (the skies under which you live) has been throwing pressure your way to get you to understand this part of your personality (this planet), this area of your attitudes toward life (this sign), this field of activities (this house of the chart), and this overall area of awareness (this quadrant) and what it needs to be defined, dsiciplined, or economized, in order that you can better move ahead. While the retrograde period lasts, it is giving you time to review exactly what has happened, how you have responded to it, and how you could better handle everything.

THE USUAL MANIFESTATION, when Saturn moves into retrograde mtoion, in a sign or in relation to a birth planet, is that the individual suddenly feels the pressure going away and he thinks, "Well, it's all over! I'm free again!" And that is precisely the most ridiculous reaction he could live out. Going forward with that attitude, he is certain to be thwarted and bewildered when Saturn resumes direct motion and the pressure comes back into effect; only then seeming (because he thought for awhile it had gone) even more intense. Many individuals, during the retrograde period, feel so relieved of the pressure that they immediately resume the haphazard way in which they were going about things before the transit began. That is certain to bring grief because THE TRANSIT IS NOT OVER. One is merely being given time to REVIEW the situation and see how he could discipline himself, define himself, or economize on his activities MORE EFFECTIVELY in this realm of himself. Do not dream, when the retrograde motion sets in that it's all over. Saturn is backing off the territory it has already covered BUT IT IS GOING TO GO RIGHT BACK OVER THAT TERRITORY as soon as direct motion resumes. In other words, something is going to be gone over twice in order to get it defined. And that's what you should be pondering. What is it that has been so difficult you are going to have two chances to handle it--and NEED those two chances?

SATURN TRANSITS A PLANET THAT IS RETROGRADE AT BIRTH. This can mean one of several things. If it is a planet from Saturn inward to the Sun, then that "part of the personality" does not work openly in the first place. It works through indirect psychic actions triggered by the unconscious. And the ability to define this part of the personality may not be in the hands of the conscious efforts of the individual at all. BUT TREMENDOUS, AND OFTEN NON-UNDERSTANDABLE PRESSURES GO ON INSIDE THE INDIVIDUAL--in there where others cannot see it or understand it. This individual (the one with the retrograde birth planetary position) can go through enormous turmoils inside that he really cannot explain to people outside. The difference between this transit, and one of a planet that is direct at birth, is often simply this: the individual with the direct planet shows his pressures and pains to the world by speaking and agonizing over them; the individual with the regrograde birth planet often goes through the same agonies without being able to communicate, in any sensible way, what is happening to him. He simply feels the pressure. He doesn't understand what it's about. Sometimes he feels so pressured that he makes lots of noises--but few of them coherently related to what is really happening inside him. For it IS happening in there more than in outer terms. A retrograde planet represents a psychic process turned inward and not manageable, except with enormous effort, by the conscious ego. A direct planet (except for Uranus, Neptune and Pluto) represents a psychic process, or part of the personality, that IS manageable by the ego consciousness (the Saturn framework of individual identity). The transit of a retrograde planet, then, often represents an unconscious process of definition that is managed not by the ego of the individual (by what the world taught him he is) but by inner voices and inner strengths (what he's becoming despite society's teaching).